Florida Real Estate Continuing Education

~~~ the FLA.CE Program ~~~

1st Edition

PERFORMANCE
PROGRAMS
COMPANY

Stephen Mettling
David Cusic
Cheryl Davis

Material in this book is not intended to represent legal advice and should not be so construed. Readers should consult legal counsel for advice regarding points of law.

© 2021 by Performance Programs Company
502 S. Fremont Ave., Suite 724, Tampa, FL 33606
info@performanceprogramscompany.com
www.performanceprogramscompany.com

ISBN: 978-0915777747

Florida Real Estate
Continuing Education (*FLA.CE*)

Table of Contents

ABOUT THE AUTHORS

Stephen Mettling. For nearly fifty years, Stephen Mettling has been actively engaged in real estate education. Beginning with Dearborn in 1972, then called Real Estate Education Company, Mr. Mettling managed the company's textbook division and author acquisitions. Subsequently he built up the company's real estate school division which eventually became the country's largest real estate, insurance and securities school network in the country. In 1978, Mr. Mettling founded Performance Programs Company, a custom training program publishing and development company specializing in commercial, industrial, and corporate real estate. Over time, Performance Programs Company narrowed its focus to real estate textbook and exam prep publishing. Currently the Company's texts and prelicense resources are used in hundreds of schools in over 48 states. As of 2021, Mr. Mettling has authored over 100 textbooks, real estate programs and exam prep manuals.

David Cusic. Dr. Cusic, an author and educator, has been engaged in vocation-oriented education since 1966. David earned his Ph.D in linguistics from Stanford University. Specializing in real estate training since 1978, he has developed numerous real estate training programs for corporate and institutional clients around the country including NAR, CoreNet Global, and the CCIM Institute.

Cheryl Davis. Cheryl Davis is a native of Cocoa Beach, Florida. She has been in the Real Estate Industry for over 35 years, and she has experience in residential and commercial sales, construction and fabrication, and property management. She is currently a broker with JoAnn P. Davis Realty, Inc.

For the past seven years, Cheryl has been an active Real Estate Instructor. Prior to that, Cheryl served as the Director of Education for the Florida Realtors Association. She is currently a co-owner of Access School of Real Estate.

One of Cheryl's specializations is as a Disability Consultant with Access Built. This organization retrofits access to homes with disabled homeowners by working with architects, developers, and contractors to develop leading-edge residential access innovations.

Cheryl has a BSBA in Human Resources, an MBA in Accounting and Leadership, and a DBA(ABD) in Industrial & Organizational Psychology.

KEY CONTRIBUTOR

Kseniya Korenva. Kseniya Korneva is a licensed REALTOR® in Tampa, Florida with a passion for writing and editing. She graduated with a Civil Engineering degree from Clemson University and fell in love with real estate shortly after. Coming from a long line of academics, her love for education runs deep. Kseniya was first introduced to the world of publishing after writing her own ebook in 2019 and realized she wanted to dive deeper. In her free time, she loves to write about personal finance and real estate on her blog (www.TheMoneyMinimalists.com).

Florida Real Estate Continuing Education (FLA.CE) Course Overview

Performance Programs Company's newly minted Florida Real Estate Continuing Education Course (the "FLACE" program) is a 14-hour course specifically designed for Florida real estate licensees and for their fulfillment of Florida's real estate continuing education requirements. As such, the course carefully complies with FREC requirements and specification for content coverage, organization length, format, and final examinations.

The thrust of the course's content is to

- provide a comprehensive yet terse review of key concepts and principles undergirding Florida brokerage and management practices
- emphasize how to develop and maintain practical yet widely-accepted standards of professional real estate practice as codified by the Realtors Code of Ethics and FREC-promulgated regulations
- highlight the more action-oriented aspects of brokerage practice as opposed to legal concepts, including risk mitigation, the basics of managing transactions, pricing property, completing contracts, financial analysis, closing, and, throughout, making conscientious and transparent disclosures.

In fulfilling these course content benchmarks, we have tried to keep the topic summaries clear, simple and relevant. Ultimately, we hope they will serve the ongoing purpose of keeping you abreast of the industry's newest trends, developments, and new evolutions.

CORE LAW

UNITS 1-3

Unit 1: License Law and Regulations Update

Unit 2: Brokerage Relationships & Licensee Disclosures

Unit 3: Brokerage Operations Regulation

UNIT 1:

LICENSE LAW AND REGULATIONS UPDATE

Unit One Learning Objectives: When the student has completed this unit he or she will be able to:

- Characterize the most essential aspects of Florida real estate licensure, including regulatory entities, types of licenses and what activities require licensure and Commission oversight.
- Summarize the requirements for initial licensure, both general and educational, for both sales associates and brokers.
- Describe the various requirements and procedures for maintaining ongoing active licensure, including the license renewal process, postlicense education requirements, and continuing education deadlines and requirements.
- Summarize the various statuses of licensure that licensees can encounter in Florida brokerage practice

LICENSE LAW SUMMARY AND PURPOSE

In the early 1900s, the Florida Legislature realized that the public needed protection when engaging in real estate transactions. Consequently, it enacted several regulations, laws, and rules to fulfill that purpose. Thus the underlying theme of all Florida real estate regulation became **consumer protection**.

A central theme of consumer protection law and regulation is disclosure. Specifically, a Florida homeowner has a duty to disclose known defects. As indicated in Chapter 455, Section 201 of Florida statutes, this ruling and subsequent rulings laid out that a seller must disclose defects if all four of the following elements are present:

> ▶ the seller has knowledge of a defect in the property
> ▶ the defect materially affects the value of the property
> ▶ the defect is not readily observable and is not known to the buyer
> ▶ the buyer establishes that the seller failed to disclose the defect

With this change of regulation, sellers are now required to disclose defects in the property whether or not the buyer asks.

Chapter 475

The primary statute encompassing Florida real estate regulation is Chapter 475. **Chapter 475** is divided into four parts and provides regulations for brokers, sales associates, appraisers, and schools. Part I created the FREC and includes its organization, powers, and duties. It also covers regulations for licensure and brokerage practices, including violations and penalties.

Part II provides regulations for appraisers. Part III is known as the Commercial Real Estate Sales Commission Lien Act and provides regulations for a broker's lien for unpaid sales commission. Part IV is known as the Commercial Real Estate Leasing Commission Lien Act and provides regulations for a broker's lien for unpaid commission earned by a lease of commercial real estate.

Chapter 455 includes the powers and duties of the DBPR and the organizational and operational requirements of the boards under the DBPR. This chapter covers general licensing provisions; education requirements; licensure examinations and testing services; disciplinary grounds, actions, procedures, and penalties; and legal and investigative services. Section 455.02 provides guidelines for licensure of members of the armed forces and their spouses.

Chapter 61J2 contains the Florida Real Estate Commission's (FREC) rules. These rules cover licensure and education requirements, non-resident licensure, brokerage operation and business practices, trust fund handling, and disciplinary matters and procedures.

Chapter 83. also known as the Florida Residential Landlord and Tenant Act, covers both residential and nonresidential tenancies. It provides regulations for rental agreements, deposits, landlord and tenant obligations, tenancy terminations, and enforcement of rights and duties.

Chapter 718 regulates condominiums and includes rights and obligations of the developers and owners' association. It establishes procedures for creating, selling, and operating condominiums.

Chapter 719 recognizes cooperatives as a form of property ownership and regulates the creation, sale, lease, and operation of cooperatives.

Chapter 760 is the Florida Civil Rights Act, which created the Florida Commission on Human Relations with the intent of protecting all individuals within Florida from discrimination based on race, color, religion, sex, pregnancy, national origin, age, handicap, or marital status.

FREC OVERVIEW AND STRUCTURE

Purpose

The Florida Real Estate Commission is the regulatory entity empowered to enforce Florida license laws. In turn, this enables the State of Florida to fulfill its mission of protecting the public. Its essential tools: education and enforcing regulatory compliance.

Composition of FREC

- 7 total members, 1 of whom must be 60 years or older
- 4 licensed brokers with active license for previous 5 years
- 1 licensed broker or licensed sales associate with active license for previous 2 years
- 2 members of the public who have never been brokers or sales associates
- All appointed by Governor for 4-year terms

Duties and powers

The principal authorized powers and duties of the FREC are to

- enact bylaws and rules for its own government
- regulate professional practices
- create and enforce license laws, rules, and regulations
- educate real estate professionals in ethical, legal, and business principles
- administer FL Real Estate Commission Education and Research Foundation
- adopt seal used to authenticate its proceedings
- establish fees for application, examination, reexamination, licensing and renewal, certification, reinstatement, and record making and keeping.
- license broker associates and sales associates, but not as general partner, member, manager, officer, or director of brokerage firm
- deny application or renewal of license, registration, or permit
- determine violations and impose penalties
- notify Division of Florida Condominiums, Timeshares, and Mobile Homes of disciplinary action against licensee

FREC limitations

FREC's regulatory and enforcement powers are administrative as opposed to criminal, i.e., FREC cannot impose criminal penalties or incarcerate license law violators or other offenders.

TYPES OF LICENSES

Florida offers real estate licenses that fall into one of three categories: broker, sales associate, and broker associate. A broker associate and a sales associate may be licensed as an individual or as a professional corporation, limited liability company, or professional limited liability company, if the individual has obtained authorization to do so from the Department of State. A broker associate and sales associate may not be licensed as a general partner, member, manager, officer, or director of a brokerage firm.

Broker

A broker is someone who is licensed to perform real estate services for another person for compensation or the expectation of compensation. Compensation can be monetary or anything else of value.

Real estate services include the sale, exchange, purchase, rental, appraisal, auction, advertising of real property, business enterprises, or business opportunities or the offer to perform any of these services. Services also include procuring sellers, buyers, lessors, or lessees.

Although a broker may "appraise" property, such appraising does not equate to appraisal services that must be performed by a registered or licensed appraiser.

The broker category of licensure also includes any individual who is a general partner, officer, or director of a partnership or corporation that acts as a broker.

Sales associate

A sales associate is someone who performs the same real estate services as a broker but who works under the direction, control, and management of a specified broker or owner-developer. A sales associate must meet additional licensure requirements to become a broker or broker associate.

Broker associate

A broker associate is someone who has obtained a broker license but performs real estate services as a sales associate under the direction, control, and management of a specified broker.

Multiple licenses

Brokers are required to hold a separate individual license for each entity or business they serve. A broker who serves multiple entities needs multiple licenses. The broker must show that the multiple licenses are necessary to conduct the brokerage business and that the licenses will not be harmful or prejudicial to anyone. Each license must be renewed separately.

Group licenses

Property owner/developers are exempt from licensure. Consequently, they employ licensed sales associates or broker associates to sell their properties. Sometimes, an owner/developer owns properties through multiple business entities with different names. When those entities are connected (for example, subsidiaries) so that they are owned or controlled by one individual or group of individuals, any licensee employed by the owner/developer may obtain a group license to be eligible to sell for all of the entities.

Remember that a sales associate or broker associate may only be employed by one broker or owner/developer at a time. The group license allows the licensee to be employed by the one owner/developer but still sell properties for multiple entities as long as they are all owned or controlled by the employing owner/developer.

LICENSED ACTIVITIES

Services requiring licensure when performed for compensation

- Selling or attempting to sell real property
- Buying or attempting to buy real property
- Leasing or attempting to lease real property
- Exchanging or attempting to exchange real property
- Negotiating or closing sale, exchange, purchase, or rental of real property or business enterprise
- Advertising or attempting to advertise real property
- Listing or selling timeshare periods

- Appraising or attempting to appraise real property
- Auctioning or attempting to auction real property
- Offering or attempting to perform real estate activities
- Procuring of sellers, purchasers, lessors, or lessees of real property or business enterprise
- Advertising or representing self as engaged in real estate services

Services not requiring licensure

- Onsite renting of apartments when employed by owner
- Owner selling timeshare period
- Renting or advertising licensed public lodging
- Tenant receiving $50 or less referral fee for referral of tenant
- Owner offering to sell real property

Exemptions from licensure requirements

- An attorney at law
- A certified public accountant
- The personal representative, receiver, trustee, or general or special magistrate appointed by will or court order
- A trustee under deed of trust or trust agreement for charitable or natural right purposes
- Any individual or entity that sells, exchanges, or leases its own real property, except if employed or compensated for that purpose
- Any salaried employee of public utility, rural electric cooperative, railroad, or state or local government agency not otherwise compensated for buying, leasing, etc. for use of employer
- Any salaried employee leasing apartments from an onsite rental office
- Any salaried manager of condominium or cooperative apartment complex renting individual units within the complex for 1 year or less
- Any compensated person or entity who performs real estate services related to radio, television, or cable enterprises regulated by the FCC, except if sale or purchase of land, buildings, fixtures, and improvements involved
- Any full-time graduate student in appraising degree program at FL college who is under direct supervision of licensed broker
- Any full or part owner of timeshare period who offers period for sale
- An exchange company for timeshare period
- Any registered, licensed, or certified appraiser or appraiser trainee performing appraisals
- Any compensated person or entity who rents or advertises public lodging establishment
- Any dealer registered under Securities and Exchange Act of 1934 or federally insured depository institution or its parent, subsidiary, or affiliate who sells, exchanges, purchases, or rents a business enterprise to accredited investor
- Any property management company or owner of apartment complex who pays referral fee of $50 or less to tenant.
- Any person selling cemetery lots
- Any person who rents mobile home or recreational vehicle park lots

INITIAL LICENSE ACQUISITION

General requirements: broker and sales associates

To qualify for a real estate license in Florida, an individual must be at least 18 years old; hold a high school diploma or its equivalent; and be honest, truthful, trustworthy, and of good character. He or she must have a good reputation for fair dealing and be competent to handle real estate transactions. Being a U.S. citizen is not a requirement for licensure as long as the individual meets all other requirements of licensure. However, applicants must have a Social Security number.

Required disclosures. An applicant must disclose any alias or also-known-as (aka) name. The applicant must also disclose whether he or she

- is under investigation for any crime or violation
- has been convicted or entered a plea of nolo contendere, no contest, or guilty for any crime
- has been denied licensure or registration for a regulated profession
- has been disciplined or is pending discipline in any jurisdiction
- has surrendered a license or had a license suspended or revoked
- has been guilty of any conduct that would be grounds for license suspension or revocation.

Broker requirements

To qualify for a broker license, the applicant must

- have a Social Security number
- submit and receive approval of the DBPR RE-2 license application
- pay all required fees
- meet all general licensure provisions including age, education, character, competency, submission of all associated background history and fingerprints

An applicant who has been licensed as a sales associate in Florida during the preceding 5 years must complete the sales associate post license education requirements, prior to applying for the broker license. This post license education requirement does not apply to applicants who hold an out-of-state sales associate license.

Experience requirement. In addition to meeting the general licensure requirements, the applicant must have held an active real estate sales associate license for at least 2 years during the 5 years prior to applying for a broker license. The applicant must also have

- worked under one or more real estate brokers who are licensed in Florida or any other U.S. state, territory, or jurisdiction or in any foreign national jurisdiction
- performed real estate services as a salaried employee of a governmental agency, or
- been licensed in any other U.S. state, territory, or jurisdiction or in any foreign national jurisdiction

Broker education requirement. A licensed sales associate who is applying for a broker license must complete the required prelicense Course II. The course includes 69 classroom hours and 3 end-of-course examination hours. The course covers the fundamentals of real estate appraising, investment, financing, and brokerage and management operations.

Sales Associate requirements

Like brokers, to qualify for a Florida sales associate license, the applicant must have a Social Security number; receive approval of the license application; meet all general licensure provisions including age, education, character, competency, submission of associated background history and fingerprints.

Education requirements. Applicants for a sales associate license must complete 63 classroom hours of an FREC-approved prelicense course, referred to as Course I, to be taken at an accredited college, career center, or registered real estate school. The course includes the fundamentals of real estate principles and practices, real estate law and license law, and associated mathematics. The required hours consist of 60 hours of instruction, either in the classroom or by way of distance learning, and three hours allowed for the end-of-course examination.

License issuance. The license is issued in an inactive status. To activate the license, the sales associate must establish an association with a broker and then either activate his or her own license by printing the DBPR RE 11 Sales Associate or Broker Sales Associate – Become Active form and having the broker sign it or by having the broker add the sales associate to the broker's online account.

The sales associate must be licensed, associated with a broker, and activated prior to performing any real estate services which require a license.

The **RE 11** form can be found online at http://www.myfloridalicense.com/dbpr/re/documents/DBPR_RE_11_Change_of_Status_Associates.pdf.

LICENSE REGISTRATION

Every person or entity who is licensed is required to register with the FREC, pay a registration fee, and submit all required information: name and address of the licensee, name and business address of the sales associate licensee's employing broker, license status of the sales associate and his or her employing broker, and whether or not the licensee is an officer, director, or partner of a real estate brokerage. Registrations must be renewed when the license is renewed.

Florida sales associates and broker associates are required to register under the employing broker and can only register under one broker at a time.

Partnerships, limited liability partnerships, limited liability companies, and corporations that act as brokers must register. Partnerships are required to license and register at least one partner as an active broker. Real estate brokerage corporations must license and register their officers and directors. Brokers must also register all branch offices.

LICENSE RENEWALS

Initial renewal – postlicense requirements

All *sales associate* licensees are required to complete a post-licensing course before the first license renewal, even if the license is inactive. The course is 45 classroom hours and includes an end-of-course examination. The course emphasizes development of skills for licensees to operate effectively and to increase public protection. Any sales associate licensee who applies for broker licensure must have completed all sales associate post-license requirements.

All *broker* licensees are required to complete post-license education which includes either one 60-hour course or two 30-hour courses and the related exams. All post-license requirements must be met prior to their first broker license renewal date.

Ongoing renewals – CE requirements

Florida real estate licenses are issued for 2-year periods, requiring renewal every 2 years. During the initial licensing period, licensees are required to complete post-licensing education based on the type of license held. During that same initial period, licensees are not required to complete continuing education, but continuing education is required for every 2-year licensing period thereafter.

During each licensing period, both active and inactive sales associates and brokers are required to complete 14 classroom hours of continuing education that must include at least 3 hours of Core Law education.

Continuing education courses may be taken in the classroom, through distance learning, or by correspondence (if the licensee qualifies for a hardship). The licensee must attend at least 90% of each of the classroom hours to receive the notice of completion. The DBPR may deny license renewal for any licensee who fails to complete continuing education requirements. Failure to provide proof of continuing education or providing false proof are grounds for disciplinary action

NONRESIDENT LICENSE REQUIREMENTS

Nonresident applicants must hold a license in their state of residency. To apply for licensure in Florida, an applicant must submit the appropriate DBPR application form for a sales associate or broker license along with the required fee, fingerprints, and any required supporting documentation, including a certification of license history issued by the state from which the applicant is claiming mutual recognition.

Mutual recognition

Mutual recognition agreements allow Florida to recognize and accept the prelicense education and experience obtained in the other state as a substitute for the requirements in the state where the nonresident is applying for a license.

The nonresident applicant must pass a written examination on general real estate law and codes with emphasis on Chapters 455 and 475 and Chapter 61J2. Only after passing the examination will the applicant be issued a Florida license. The nonresident licensee is then responsible for completing all post-license and continuing education that is required of a Florida licensee.

Florida licensees may seek licensure in any state that has a mutual recognition agreement with Florida, keeping in mind that each state may have different requirements for nonresident licensure. To apply for a nonresident license, the Florida licensee should contact the other state's real estate commission.

LICENSE STATUSES

Active status

Sales associate or broker licenses are initially issued on inactive status. Since licensees are allowed to practice real estate only if their licenses are on active status, they must activate their licenses before they offer or provide real estate services. Their licenses must also be on active status before the licensee can accept commission or other fees for a real estate service.

A sales associate can activate the license by registering under an employing broker or by having the employing broker activate the license through the broker's online account. Anyone who practices without an active status license is violating license law and may be disciplined.

Voluntary inactive status

There are multiple ways a license may become voluntarily inactive: the licensee does not activate the license when it is initially issued; the licensee chooses to renew an active license on inactive status; or a licensee requests the DBPR place the license on inactive status. Most often, licensees choose voluntary inactive status because they have decided not to practice real estate for a period of time.

When a license is in voluntary inactive status, the licensee may reactivate the license at any time by applying to the DBPR, paying a reactivation fee, and meeting all post-license or continuing education requirements.

Just as with active licenses, voluntarily inactive licenses must be renewed every 2 years to remain valid. The inactive licensee needs to apply for renewal on inactive status, complete 12 hours of continuing education for each year the license was inactive, and pay the renewal fee.

Involuntary inactive status

If the licensee does not renew the active or voluntarily inactive license by the expiration date, the license status automatically becomes involuntarily inactive. The license is also deemed delinquent.

The DBPR will send a notice of involuntary inactive status at least 90 days prior to the license expiration date. If a broker's license is suspended or revoked, all sales associates and broker associates registered under that broker will automatically become involuntarily inactive. Their licenses will remain in that status until the broker is again reinstated or until they register under a new broker.

If these licensees decide not to practice real estate, they may change their licenses' involuntarily inactive status to voluntarily inactive through their online DBPR account.

Once in involuntarily inactive status for nonrenewal, the license can be renewed if the licensee applies to the DBPR, pays the renewal fee for each year the license was involuntarily inactive plus any associated late fees, and completes the required continuing education based on the time frame of inactive status.

The licensee can renew as either active or voluntarily inactive but must do so within 2 years of becoming involuntarily inactive. If the licensee fails to renew during the 2 years, the license automatically expires and becomes null and void.

Null and void license status

Null and void licenses are those that no longer exist unless they are reactivated via the following allowable conditions. A license may become null and void under any of the following conditions.

- The sales associate does not complete post-license education prior to the renewal date for the initial licensure period.
  To reengage in real estate activities, the individual must requalify for licensure by retaking the prelicensure education and exams and passing the state examination.
- A licensee on involuntary inactive status does not renew the license within 2 years of becoming involuntarily inactive.
  The FREC may reinstate this license if the individual applies to the Commission within 6 months of becoming null and void, shows proof of a physical or financial hardship, completes continuing education, and pays all required fees.
- A license is revoked for disciplinary reasons.
  Revoked licenses may never be reinstated, and the individual may never reapply for licensure.
- A licensee relinquishes the license unrelated to any disciplinary actions or investigations.
  The licensee must notify the DBPR of the intent to relinquish the license.

Notifications

A broker must notify the Commission within 10 days of any business address change. Until the Commission is notified of the address change, the broker's license ceases to be in force. While the license is in active status, the broker may not engage in real estate activities.

===

SNAPSHOT REVIEW: UNIT ONE

LICENSE LAW AND REGULATIONS UPDATE

LICENSE LAW SUMMARY AND PURPOSE

- The underlying theme of all Florida real estate regulation is consumer protection
- Seller must disclose all known material defects
- Chapter 475 discusses the regulations for brokers, sales associates, appraisers and schools
- Chapter 455 includes the powers and duties of the DBPR and the organizational and operational requirements of the boards under the DBPR
- Chapter 61J2 contains the Florida Real Estate Commission's (FREC) rules
- Chapter 83 covers residential and nonresidential tenancies
- Chapter 718 establishes procedures for creating, selling, and operating condominiums
- Chapter 719 regulates the creation, sale, lease, and operation of cooperatives
- Chapter 760 protects all individuals within Florida from discrimination based on race, color, religion, sex, pregnancy, national origin, age, handicap, or marital status

FREC OVERVIEW AND STRUCTURE

- FREC rules regulate licensure; education requirements, non-resident licensure, brokerage operation and business practices; trust fund handling; and disciplinary matters, procedures
- FREC composed of 7 members. 4 licensed brokers, 1 licensed broker or licensed sales associate, and 2 members of the public who have never been licensed
- All members are appointed by Governor for 4-year terms

TYPES OF LICENSES

- A broker is licensed to perform real estate services for another person for compensation
- A sales associate performs the same real estate services as a broker but who works under the direction, control, and management of a specified broker or owner-developer
- A broker associate is someone who has obtained a broker licensed but performs real estate services as a sales associate under a specified broker
- A broker who serves multiple entities needs multiple licenses
- Group licenses allow the licensee to be employed by an owner/developer but still sell properties for multiple entities as long as they are all owned or controlled by the employing owner/developer

LICENSED ACTIVITIES

- Selling or buying real property
- Leasing, exchanging , negotiating or closing sale, exchange, purchase, or rental of real property or business enterprise
- Advertising real property
- Listing or selling timeshare periods

- Appraising or auctioning real property
- Offering or attempting to perform real estate activities
- Procuring sellers, purchasers, lessors, or lessees of real property or business enterprise
- Advertising or representing self as engaged in real estate services

Exemptions from license requirements
- An attorney at law, certified public accountant, personal representative, receiver, trustee, or general or special magistrate appointed by will or court order
- A trustee under deed of trust,
- Any individual or entity that sells, exchanges, or leases its own real property
- Any salaried employee of public utility, rural electric cooperative, railroad, or state or local government agency; any salaried employee leasing apartments from an onsite rental office
- Any salaried manager of condominium or cooperative apartment complex renting individual units within the complex for 1 year or less
- Any compensated person or entity who performs real estate services related to radio, television, or cable enterprises regulated by the FCC, except if sale or purchase of land, buildings, fixtures, and improvements involved
- Any full or part owner of timeshare period who offers period for sale
- Any registered, licensed, or certified appraiser or appraiser trainee performing appraisals
- Any compensated person or entity who rents or advertises public lodging establishment
- Any property management company or owner of apartment complex who pays referral fee of $50 or less to tenant
- Any person selling cemetery lots
- Any person who rents mobile homes or recreational vehicle park lots

INITIAL LICENSE ACQUISITION

General requirements: broker and sales associates
- submit to background check, provide fingerprints; provide information about criminal history
- DBPR to approve or deny application within 90 days of receipt; applicant has right to appeal denial
- application valid for 2 years; prelicense course valid for 2 years for licensure exam
- exempt: attorneys; those with 4-year real estate degrees; those with mutual recognition agreement
- applicants must disclose aliases; whether under investigation; if ever convicted of a crime; if ever denied licensure; if any discipline is pending; if ever lost license

Broker requirements
- SS number, application approval, fees paid, meet age, education, character, competency, background requirements; complete sales associate post license education
- active sales associate license for 2 years within past 5 years; worked under broker within 2 years of course completion; failures may retake exam unlimited times; may review incorrect answers issued as inactive; activate by filing form

Sales associate requirements
- SS number, application approval, fees paid, meet age, education, character, competency, background requirements
- 60-hour course, 3-hour exam with 70% pass score
- within 2 years of course completion; pass with 75% score; print and activate license

- retake failed exam unlimited times; may review incorrect answers
- license issued in inactive status; licensee must associate with broker before performing services

LICENSE REGISTRATION

- all licensees must register with FREC, submit identification, license information; status
- must renew registrations along with license; can only register under one broker; business entities and branches must also register

LICENSE RENEWALS

Initial renewal - postlicense requirements
- renew for 2-year periods; initial period 18-24 months; renew March 31 or September 30; complete post-license or continuing education; involuntary inactive status for nonrenewal
- sales associates – 45-hour postlicense course; must pass course exam with 75% score
- brokers – 60-hour course and end-of-course exam with 75% pass score

Ongoing- CE requirements
- Postlicense: sales associates – 45-hour course and end-of-course exam with 75% pass score
- Postlicense: brokers -60-hour course and end-of-course exam with 75% pass score
- Continuing education: 14 hours every 2-year license period to include 3 hours of Core Law & 3 hours of Business Ethics
- License reactivation: involuntary inactive status for 12-24 months can reactivate with 28-hour course and exam with 70% pass score
- 14 hours every 2-year license period to include 3 hours of Core Law & 3 hours of Business Ethics
- involuntary inactive status for 12-24 months can reactivate with 28-hour course and exam with 70% pass score

NONRESIDENT LICENSE REQUIREMENTS

- hold license in resident state; submit certificate of license history; meet FL application requirements

Mutual recognition
- agreement of FL and another state to recognize other state's prelicense education and require laws and rules exam

LICENSE STATUSES

Active
- active required for practicing

Inactive
- voluntary inactive when initial license not activated, when licensee chooses status at renewal, when licensee requests; reactivate by applying, paying fee, completing CE; renew every 2 years
- involuntary inactive for nonrenewal; reactivate by applying, paying fee, completing CE, all within 2 years of involuntary inactive status
- null and void for not completing post-license course, for not renewing involuntary inactive license within 2 years, for revoked license, for voluntary license relinquish

Changing status
- ceases to be in force when business address changes; must report within 10 days

Notifications
- licensee to notify DBPR of current mailing address or change of address within 10 days
- FL resident licensee becoming nonresident to notify FREC within 60 days

Check Your Understanding Quiz:

Unit One: License Law and Regulations Update

Carefully read each question then provide your best answer based on what you learned in this unit. Then check your answers against the Answer Key which immediately follows the quiz questions.

1. Which of the following individuals is NOT required to hold a Florida real estate license?

    a. An appraiser
    b. Someone who is helping a tenant find a property to lease
    c. A trustee acting under a deed of trust
    d. A person advertising their neighbor's home for sale

2. How long are licenses issued for?

    a. 2 years
    b. 1 year
    c. 3 years
    d. 7 years

3. What is the post-licensing requirement for sales associates?

    a. Sales associates must complete a 14 hour post-licensing course before the first license renewal.
    b. Sales associates must complete a 45 hour post-licensing course before the first license renewal.
    c. Sales associates must complete a 60 hour post-licensing course before the first license renewal.
    d. Sales associates must complete a 90 hour post-licensing course before the first license renewal.

4. Which of the following is exempt from post-license education requirements?

    a. Brokers
    b. Sales associates
    c. Appraisers
    d. Licensees with a four-year degree in real estate from an accredited university

5. What is the minimum age requirement for a Florida licensee?

    a. 21
    b. 25
    c. 18
    d. There is no minimum age requirement.

6. If an applicant fails the licensing exam, how long must he or she wait before taking it again?

   a. 14 days
   b. 30 days
   c. 6 months
   d. There is no waiting period to retake the examination.

==

Answer Key:

Unit One: License Law and Regulations Update

1. **c. A trustee acting under a deed of trust.**
2. **a. 2 years**
3. **b. Sales associates must complete a 45 hour post-licensing course before the first license renewal.**
4. **d. Licensees with a four-year degree in real estate from an accredited university**
5. **c. 18**
6. **d. There is no waiting period to retake the examination.**

==

UNIT 2:

BROKERAGE RELATIONSHIPS AND LICENSEE DISCLOSURES

Unit Two Learning Objectives: When the student has completed this unit he or she will be able to:

- Describe the various forms of agency relationship allowed by Florida law, and how each relationship varies in form and duties.
- Summarize relationship disclosure requirements by type of relationship imposed by the Brokerage Relationship Disclosure Act.
- List and summarize the various non-relationship disclosures that licensees and/or sellers must conduct in a timely fashion, including those relating to property condition, the environment, material facts, and homeowners associations.
- Summarize the forms, liabilities and pitfalls of misrepresentation including intentional and negligent misrepresentation.

THE BROKERAGE RELATIONSHIP DISCLOSURE ACT

Under the Brokerage Relationship Disclosure Act, all real estate transactions impose certain duties and obligations on licensees. Written disclosures, however, are required only when a brokerage is acting as a single agent or in a no-brokerage relationship in a residential sale transaction.

Residential sale transactions are those involving

- improved residential properties with four or fewer dwelling units
- unimproved residential properties zoned for four or fewer residential units
- agricultural properties of ten acres or less

No written disclosure is needed when the brokerage is acting as a transaction broker, as this relationship is the default presumed under Florida law.

TYPES OF BROKERAGE RELATIONSHIP

Single Agency Relationships

Here, the agent represents one party in a transaction. The client may be either seller or buyer.

Seller agency. In the traditional situation, a seller or landlord is the agent's client. A buyer or tenant is the customer.

Buyer agency. Recently, it has become common for an agent to represent a buyer or tenant. In this relationship, the property buyer or tenant is the client and the property owner is the customer.

Dual agency. Here, an agency relationship is established with a brokerage firm and not with any one agent within the firm. Therefore, a dual agency would exist if one agent within the firm represented the seller while another agent in the same firm represented the buyer. Dual agency as a form of representation is prohibited in Florida whether it is disclosed or not disclosed.

Subagency. In subagency, a broker associate or sales associate works as the agent of a broker who is the agent of a buyer or seller. In effect, the associate, as agent of the broker, is the subagent of the client. The subagent owes the same duties to the broker's client as the broker does.

Single agency duties. The duties of the single agent are enumerated in the single agent's notice to buyers and sellers (following section). To wit, these are

- *As a single agent, (insert name of Real Estate Entity and its Associates) owe to you the following duties:*
- *Dealing honestly and fairly;*
- *Loyalty;*
- *Confidentiality;*
- *Obedience;*
- *Full disclosure;*
- *Accounting for all funds;*
- *Skill, care, and diligence in the transaction;*
- *Presenting all offers and counteroffers in a timely manner, unless a party has previously directed the licensee otherwise in writing; and*
- *Disclosing all known facts that materially affect the value of residential real property and are not readily observable.*

Transaction broker relationships

Florida prohibits both parties to a transaction from being represented by the same brokerage in a dual agency relationship. Instead, the transaction broker relationship was created to allow a single brokerage to provide limited representation and duties to both the seller and the buyer in the same transaction. Limited representation means neither party is responsible for the licensee's actions.

In a transaction broker relationship, the broker does not represent either party in a fiduciary capacity or as a single agent. Neither party has the right of the licensee's undivided loyalty. Further, because the broker is not representing either one of the parties as a client, then all parties to the transaction are considered customers.

Florida law makes the presumption that all licensees are operating as transaction brokers unless the broker and the customer have entered into a written single agent or nonrepresentation agreement. Consequently, transaction brokers are not required to provide customers with a transaction broker relationship notice or disclosure.

Duties of a transaction broker. As with any Florida agency relationship, the broker must disclose the duties owed to both parties.

- dealing honestly and fairly
- accounting for all funds

- using skill, care, and diligence in the transaction
- disclosing all known material facts that are not readily observable and that affect the property's value
- presenting all offers and counteroffers in a timely manner unless directed otherwise
- providing limited confidentiality unless either party waives in writing
- performing any additional duties agreed upon by both parties

Duties not imposed on the transaction broker. Since there are no fiduciary duties binding the transaction broker, the broker is held to standards for dealing with *customers* as opposed to clients. These include honesty, fair dealing, and reasonable care. The transaction broker is under no obligation to inspect the property for the benefit of a party or verify the accuracy of statements made by a party.

Nonrepresentation relationships

A licensee may enter into a listing agreement with a seller and be paid a commission or other compensation while having no brokerage relationship with buyer or seller. In this situation, the licensee owes no loyalty or other fiduciary duties to either party but still owes certain duties to the party or parties as customers. Those duties must be disclosed in writing before the licensee shows a property.

BROKERAGE RELATIONSHIP DISCLOSURES

Under Florida's Brokerage Relationship Disclosure Act, licensees may establish a relationship with a buyer or seller as either a transaction broker or as a single agent. The licensee may also assist a buyer or seller with no brokerage relationship, known as nonrepresentation. The relationship established must be disclosed in writing to the involved parties. The licensee may transition from one type of relationship to the other type with the consent of the buyer and/or seller and with the disclosure of the duties owed to the client or customer under the new relationship.

The customer is not required to enter into any brokerage relationship with a licensee.

Disclosure notice: no brokerage relationship

NO BROKERAGE RELATIONSHIP NOTICE

FLORIDA LAW REQUIRES THAT REAL ESTATE LICENSEES WHO HAVE NO BROKERAGE RELATIONSHIP WITH A POTENTIAL SELLER OR BUYER DISCLOSE THEIR DUTIES TO SELLERS AND BUYERS.

As a real estate licensee who has no brokerage relationship with you, (insert name of Real Estate Entity and its Associates) owe to you the following duties:

1. *Dealing honestly and fairly.*
2. *Disclosing all known facts that materially affect the value of the residential property that are not readily observable to the buyer.*
3. *Accounting for all funds entrusted to the licensee.*

Disclosure notice: single agency relationship

SINGLE AGENT NOTICE

FLORIDA LAW REQUIRES THAT REAL ESTATE LICENSEES OPERATING AS SINGLE AGENTS DISCLOSE TO BUYERS AND SELLERS THEIR DUTIES.

1. *As a single agent, (insert name of Real Estate Entity and its Associates) owe to you the following duties:*
2. *Dealing honestly and fairly;*
3. *Loyalty;*
4. *Confidentiality;*
5. *Obedience;*
6. *Full disclosure;*
7. *Accounting for all funds;*
8. *Skill, care, and diligence in the transaction;*
9. *Presenting all offers and counteroffers in a timely manner, unless a party has previously directed the licensee otherwise in writing; and*
10. *Disclosing all known facts that materially affect the value of residential real property and are not readily observable.*

SELLER'S PROPERTY CONDITION DISCLOSURE

Florida requires sellers to make a written disclosure about property condition to a prospective buyer. This seller disclosure may or may not relieve the agent of some liabilities for disclosure. The **Residential Property Condition Disclosure** is the seller's written summary of the property's condition at the time of contracting for sale. The disclosure is entered on state-approved forms.

Owner's role

State legislation requires owners of previously occupied single family homes and buildings containing 1-4 dwelling units to provide the disclosure to prospective buyers if they are selling, exchanging, or optioning their property. The disclosure must be transmitted to the prospective buyer no later than when the buyer makes an offer.

A typical form requires the seller to affirm whether or not problems exist in any of the listed features and systems of the property. In denying that a problem exists, the seller claims to have no knowledge of a defect. If a defect does in fact exist, the seller can be held liable for intentional misrepresentation. A third possible response to a property condition question is that of "no representation." Here, the seller makes no claim of knowledge as to whether a problem exists. With this answer, the seller is no longer held liable for a disclosure of any kind relating to a particular feature, whether a defect is known or otherwise.

Once the seller has signed the form and delivered it to the buyer, the buyer must acknowledge receipt and knowledge of the property condition disclosures, along with other provisions set forth on the form.

Licensee's role

The residential property re-seller must comply with the property condition disclosure requirement whether an agent is employed in the transaction or not. If an agent is involved in the transaction, the agent must disclose any and all material facts he or she knows or should reasonably know about the property, regardless of what the seller may have disclosed on the form.

Right of rescission

Sellers who fail to complete and deliver the property condition disclosure statement to buyers in a timely fashion effectively give the buyer a subsequent right under certain conditions to rescind the sale contract and re-claim their deposits. The buyer must follow certain procedures and meet certain deadlines in order to legitimately effect the cancellation. The buyer's right to cancel persists until closing or occupancy, whichever comes first.

Seller's Property Condition Disclosure Form

The following exhibit is part of a typical property condition disclosure form showing the level of detail that is expected in a seller's disclosure.

Buyers and seller should be aware that any agreement executed between the parties will supercede this form as to any abligations on the part of the seller to repair items identified below and/or the obligation of the buyer to accept such items "as is".

INSTRUCTIONS TO THE SELLER

Complete this form yourself and answer each question to the best of your knowledge. If an answer is an estimate, clearly label it as such. The Seller hereby authorizes any agent(s) representing any party in this transaction to provide a copy of this statement to any person or entity in connection with any actual or anticipated sale of the subject property.

PROPERTY ADDRESS _____ CITY _____
SELLER'S NAMES(S) _____ PROPERTY AGE _____
DATE SELLER ACQUIRED THE PROPERTY_____ DO YOU OCCUPY THE PROPERTY? _____
IF NOT OWNER-OCCUPIED. HOW LONG HAS IT BEEN SINCE THE SELLER OCCUPIED THE PROPERTY? _____
(Check the one that applies) THIS PROPERTY IS A ☐ SITE BUILT HOME ☐ NONSITE BUILT HOME

☐ Range   ☐ Central Air Conditioning   ☐ Garage Door Opener(s)
☐ Oven   ☐ Wall/Window Air Conditioning   ☐ (Number of openers _____)
☐ Microwave   ☐ Window Screens   ☐ Intercom
☐ Dishwasher   ☐ Rain Gutters   ☐ TV Antenna/Satellite Dish
☐ Garbage Disposal   ☐ Fireplace(s) (Number _____) ☐ Pool
☐ Trash Compactor   ☐ Gas Starter for Fireplace   ☐ Spa/Whirlpool Tub
☐ Water Softener Alarm   ☐ Smoke Detector/Fire   ☐ Hot Tub
☐ 220 Volt Wiring   ☐ Burglar Alarm   ☐ Sauna
☐ Washer/Dryer Hookups   ☐ Patio/Decking/Gazebo   ☐ Current Termite Contract
☐ Central Heating   ☐ Irrigation System   ☐ Access to Public Streets
☐ Heat Pump   ☐ Sump Pump   ☐ Other_____
                                                                  ☐ Other_____

Garage:	☐ Attached	☐ Not Attached	☐ Carport	
Water Heater:	☐ Gas	☐ Solar	☐ Electric	
Water Supply:	☐ City	☐ Well	☐ Private Utility	Other_____
Waste Disposal:	☐ City Sewer	☐ Septic Tank	☐ Other _____	
Gas Supply:	☐ Utility	☐ Bottled	☐ Other _____	

Roof(s): Type _____ Age(approx) _____
Other Items: _____

To the best of your knowledge, are any of the above NOT in operating condition?   ☐ YES   ☐ NO
If YES, then describe (Attach additional sheets if necessary);

ARE YOU (SELLER) AWARE OF ANY DEFECTS/AMLFUNCTIONS IN ANY OF THE FOLLOWING?

	YES	NO	UNKNOWN		YES	NO	UNKNOWN
Interior Walls	☐	☐	☐	Central Heating	☐	☐	☐
Ceilings	☐	☐	☐	Central Air Conditioning	☐	☐	☐
Floors	☐	☐	☐	Electrical System	☐	☐	☐
Windows	☐	☐	☐	Exterior Walls	☐	☐	☐
Doors	☐	☐	☐	Roof	☐	☐	☐
Insulation	☐	☐	☐	Basement	☐	☐	☐
Plumbing	☐	☐	☐	Foundation	☐	☐	☐
Sewer/Septic	☐	☐	☐	Slab	☐	☐	☐
Heat Pump	☐	☐	☐	Driveway	☐	☐	☐
				Sidewalks	☐	☐	☐

If any of the above is/are marked YES, Please explain:
_____
_____
_____

This Form Compliments of Kirkland, Rothman-Branning & Associates, PLLC   ww. kr-ba.com
901-758-558   jtk10-02

C. ARE YOU (SELLER) AWARE OF ANY OF THE FOLLOWING?

	YES	NO	UNKNOWN
1. Substances, materials, or products which may be an environmental hazard such as, but not limited to: asbestos, radon gas, lead-based paint, fuel or chemical storage tanks, and/or contaminated water on the subject property	☐	☐	☐
2. Features shared in common with adjoining landowners, such as, but not limited to, walls, fences, and driveways, whose use or responsibility for maintenance may have an effect on the subject property	☐	☐	☐
3. Any authorized changes in roads, drainage, or utilities affecting the property, or contiguous to the property	☐	☐	☐
4. Any changes since the most recent survey of this property was done	☐	☐	☐
Most recent survey of the property: _____ [check here ☐ if unknown]			
5. Any encroachments, easements, or similar items that may affect your ownership interest in the property	☐	☐	☐
6. Room additions, structural modifications, or other alterations or repairs made without necessary permits	☐	☐	☐
7. Room additions, structural modifications, or other alterations or repairs not in compliance with building codes	☐	☐	☐
8. Is heating and air conditioning supplied to all finished rooms?	☐	☐	☐
If the same type of system is not used for all finished rooms, please explain. _____			
9. Landfill (compacted or otherwise) on the property or any portion thereof	☐	☐	☐
10. Any settling from any cause, or slippage, sliding, or other soil problems	☐	☐	☐
11. Flooding, drainage, or grading problems	☐	☐	☐
12. Any requirement that flood insurance be maintained on the property	☐	☐	☐
13. Property or structural damage from fire, water, wind, storm, earthquake/tremor, landslide or wood destroying organisms	☐	☐	☐
14. Any zoning violations, nonconforming uses, and/or violations of "setback" requirements	☐	☐	☐
15. Neighborhood noise problems or other nuisances	☐	☐	☐
16. Subdivisions and/or deed restrictions or obligations	☐	☐	☐
17. A Homeowners Association (HOA) which has any authority over the subject property	☐	☐	☐
Name of HOA: _____			
HOA Address: _____			
Monthly Dues: _____ Special Assessments: _____			
18. Any "common area" (facilities such as, but not limited to, pools, tennis courts, walkways, or other areas co-owned in undivided interest with others)	☐	☐	☐
19. Any notices of abatement or citations against the property	☐	☐	☐
20. Any lawsuit(s) or proposed lawsuit(s) by or against the seller which affect or will affect the property	☐	☐	☐
21. Is any system, equipment or part of the property being leased	☐	☐	☐
If yes, please explain, and include a written statement regarding payment information.			
22. Any exterior wall covering of the structure covered with exterior insulation and finishing systems (EIFS), also known as "synthetic stucco"	☐	☐	☐
If yes, has there been a recent inspection to determine whether the structure has excessive moisture accumulation and/or moisture related damage? (The Tennessee Real Estate Commission urges any buyer or seller who encounters this product to have a qualified professional inspect the structure in question for the preceding concern and provide a written report of their finding.)	☐	☐	☐
If yes, please explain. If necessary, please attach an additional sheet.			

D. CERTIFICATION:
I/we certify that the information herein, concerning the real property located at _____, is true and correct to the best of my/our knowledge as of the date signed. Should any of these conditions change prior to conveyance of title to this property, these changes will be disclosed in addendum(a) to this document.

_____ _____
Transferor (Seller)   Date

_____ _____
Transferor (Seller)   Date

Parties may wish to obtain professional advice and/or inspections of the property and to negotiate appropriate provisions in the purchase agreement regarding advice, inspections, or defects.

TRANSFEREE/BUYER'S ACKNOWLEDGMENT: I/we understand that this disclosure statement is not intended as a substitute for any inspection, and that I/we have a responsibility to pay diligent attention to and inquire about those material defects which are evident by careful observation.

I/we acknowledge receipt of a copy of this disclosure.

_____ _____
Transferee (Buyer)   Date

_____ _____
Transferee (Buyer)   Date

ENVIRONMENTAL DISCLOSURES

Licensees are expected to be aware of environmental issues and to know where to look for professional help. They are not expected to have expert knowledge of environmental law nor of physical conditions in a property. Rather, they must treat potential environmental hazards in the same way that they treat other material facts about a property: disclosure. It is advisable to have an attorney draft the appropriate disclosures to lessen the broker's liability should problems occur in the future.

Lead paint

The Lead-based Paint Act of 1992 requires a seller or seller's agent to disclose known lead problems in properties built before 1978. The licensee must give the buyer or lessee a copy of the EPA-HUD-US Consumer Product Safety Commission booklet, "Protect Your Family from Lead in your home."

Further, the 1996 lead-based paint regulation requires sellers or lessors of almost all residential properties built before 1978 to disclose known lead-based paint hazards and provide any relevant records available. The seller is not required to test for lead but must allow the buyer a ten-day period for lead inspection. Only a licensed lead professional is permitted to deal with testing, removal or encapsulation. It is the real estate practitioner's responsibility to ensure compliance.

CERCLA

Under CERCLA and the Superfund Amendment of 1986, current landowners as well as previous owners of a property may be held liable for environmental violations, even if "innocent" of a violation. Sellers often carry the greatest exposure, and real estate licensees may be held liable for improper disclosure.

Additional environmental disclosures

Mold. The presence of mold in the home must be disclosed as a latent defect. Flooding and water damage must also be disclosed as both of those can lead to mold growth. Inspections do not always find mold because it often grows inside walls and ductwork. Most molds require removal by a professional.

Asbestos. While harmless in its original condition, it can cause lung cancer if its dust filters into the air. If it is found in a home during remodeling, it must be removed by professionals to prevent contamination. It can be found in roofing and siding, older insulation, textured paint, artificial ashes sold for gas fireplaces, some vinyl floor tiles, coatings for older hot water and steam pipes

Faulty septic systems. Inspections of septic systems are important because these systems take wastewater from the property, remove most of the contaminants, and then put the water into the soil. If the system is faulty, it can be releasing contaminated water into the soil, thereby contaminating the soil. Potential buyers and septic system users should have the county health department conduct an inspection of the system.

Illegal drug manufacturing. Manufacturing illegal drugs such as methamphetamine produces highly toxic fumes that last a long time. Any property suspected as having been a place for drug manufacturing should be investigated prior to being sold or leased, and the possible health hazards must be disclosed to the potential buyer or renter.

Leaking underground storage tanks. USTs have at least 10 percent of their volume underground and are used to store fuel oil, gasoline, and other toxic fluids. Tanks made of steel can corrode over time and leak their contents into the surrounding soil, contaminating groundwater. Potential buyers must be informed of the presence of a UST on the property and of the health and financial risks of purchasing a property that contains a UST

Safe Drinking Water Act. Congress passed the Safe Drinking Water Act (SDWA) in 1974 (amended 1986 and 1996) to regulate and protect the public supply of drinking water. Property sellers generally must disclose the source of drinking water for the property and the presence, type and location of any septic system on the property. A water supply other than a municipal one and any septic system other than a standard one should be tested

LICENSEE DISCLOSURES

Florida licensees are obligated to the duty of full disclosure with clients. This includes the duty to inform the client of all material facts, reports, and rumors that might affect the client's interests in the property transaction.

In recent years, the disclosure standard has been raised to require an agent to disclose items that a practicing agent should know, whether the agent actually had the knowledge or not, and regardless of whether the disclosure furthers or impedes the progress of the transaction.

By contrast, there is no obligation to obtain or disclose information related to a customer's race, creed, color, religion, sex or national origin: anti-discrimination laws hold such information to be immaterial to the transaction. As a general rule, licensees should focus disclosures on specific, required relationship disclosures and property condition disclosures – not on statements that characterize the people who occupy or should occupy the property.

Florida law requires a seller to make a written disclosure about property condition to a prospective buyer.

Selling with an interest

Whenever a licensee owns an interest in a property that he or she will be buying or selling, the licensee is required to disclose his or her licensed status to all prospective sellers and buyers. This disclosure must be made in a timely fashion such that the principals are not misled in any negotiation process.

Material facts disclosure

Licensees are obligated to disclose all material facts to clients. Generally, a material fact is any fact that will have an impact on the seller's decision making process. Material facts can be largely classified as either relating to agency disclosure, property condition and environmental hazards, or the buyer.

Critical material facts for disclosure include:

- the agent's opinion of the property's condition

- information about the buyer's motivations and financial qualifications

- discussions between agent and buyer regarding the possibility of the agent's representing the buyer in another transaction.

- adverse material facts, including property condition, title defects, environmental hazards, and property defects

MISREPRESENTATION

Any licensee who fails to live up to prevailing standards of disclosure may be held liable for negligence, fraud, or violation of state real estate license laws and regulations. Brokers and sales associates should be particularly careful about intentional or negligent misrepresentation and offering inappropriate expert advice when working with customers.

Intentional misrepresentation

A licensee may intentionally or unintentionally defraud a buyer by misrepresenting or concealing facts. While it is acceptable to promote the features of a property to a buyer or the virtues of a buyer to a seller, it is a fine line that divides promotion from misrepresentation. Silent misrepresentation, which is intentionally failing to reveal a material fact, is just as fraudulent as a false statement.

Negligent misrepresentation

A licensee can be held liable for failure to disclose facts the agent was not aware of if it can be demonstrated that the licensee should have known such facts. For example, if it is a common standard that licensees inspect property, then one can be held liable for failing to disclose a leaky roof that was not inspected.

Misrepresentation of expertise

A licensee should not act or speak outside that person's area of expertise. A customer may rely on anything an agent says, and the agent will be held accountable. For example, a licensee represents that a property will appreciate. The buyer interprets this as expert investment advice and buys the property. If the property does not appreciate, the buyer may hold the sales associate or broker liable.

===

32

SNAPSHOT REVIEW: UNIT TWO

BROKERAGE RELATIONSHIPS AND LICENSEE DISCLOSURES

THE BROKERAGE RELATIONSHIP DISCLOSURE ACT

- all transactions impose duties on licensees
- disclosures required in single agent or no-brokerage relationship for residential transactions
- no disclosure needed when acting as transaction broker

TYPES OF BROKERAGE RELATIONSHIPS

Single agency relationships
- licensee represents one party
- seller or buyer agency – seller or buyer, respectively is the client
- dual agency – relationship in the brokerage firm, not a single licensee; one licensee in firm represents seller; another represents buyer; dual agency as a form of representation is prohibited in Florida – see transaction broker relationships
- subagency -- broker associate or sales associate works as the agent of a broker who is the agent of a buyer or seller
- single agency duties – honesty; fairness; loyalty; confidentiality; obedience; full disclosure; accounting for all funds; skill, care and diligence; presenting all offers; disclosing material facts

Transaction broker relationships
- allows a single brokerage go provide limited representation where neither party is responsible for the licensee's actions
- broker does not operate in a fiduciary capacity; both principals are considered customers
- Florida law presumes all licensees operate as transaction brokers unless there is a written single agent or nonrepresentation agreement
- duties: honesty, fairness; accounting; skill, care, diligence; disclosing material facts; presenting all offers; providing limited confidentiality; performing duties as agreed upon
- transaction brokers not bound to inspect the property or verify accuracy of representations

Nonrepresentation relationships
- licensee can enter into relationship with seller while having no brokerage relationship with buyer or seller – licensee owes no loyalty to either party; must disclose what duties will be discharged

BROKERAGE RELATIONSHIP DISCLOSURES

- duties, not representation choices
- separate forms for each representation type
- FL Brokerage Relationship Disclosure Act allows transaction broker, single agent, and nonrepresentation
- must disclose duties of each relationship
- honesty and fair dealing; exercise of reasonable care and skill; proper disclosures; danger areas: misrepresentation; advising beyond expertise

- Under the Brokerage Relationship Disclosure Act, all real estate transactions impose certain duties and obligations on licensees.

SELLERS PROPERTY CONDITION DISCLOSURE

- written seller disclosure may be required; may or may not relieve agent of some liabilities
- seller discloses known problems; agent discloses known material facts known or should have known; failure to disclose grants right of rescission to buyer
- agent should advise seller of red flag issues detected; may include environmental concerns, property size and shape, neighborhood, construction quality, flooding, floorplan, adjacent property

ENVIRONMENTAL DISCLOSURES

- duties of detecting, disclosing, remediating for owner and agent vary; typically include: lead-based paint, mold, asbestos, air quality, water quality, carbon monoxide, septic system, drug manufacturing, radon, formaldehyde, underground tanks
- agents need to be familiar with requirements of EPA, CERCLA/Superfund Act, Clean Air and Water Acts, Lead-based Paint Act, among others
- licensees must be aware of issues, know where to find professional help, disclose
- agents should inform clients of limitations of home warranties; not a substitute for inspection
- inspections can reveal structural, electrical, plumbing, roof, foundation, pest, environmental issues; agent must disclose inspection results if known

LICENSEE DISCLOSURES

Selling with an interest
- licensees must disclose licensed status if transacting owned property

Material facts
- Licensees are obligated to disclose all material facts to clients; material fact – property condition affecting value

MISREPRESENTATION

- Any licensee who fails to live up to prevailing standards of disclosure may be held liable for negligence, fraud, or violation of state real estate license laws and regulations
- Intentional representation occurs when a licensee defrauds a buyer by misrepresenting or concealing facts
- Negligent misrepresentation occurs when a licensee fails to disclose facts that he or she should have known
- A licensee should not act or speak outside of their area of expertise. This is called misrepresentation of expertise

Check Your Understanding Quiz:

Unit Two: Brokerage Relationships and Licensee Disclosures

Carefully read each question then provide your best answer based on what you learned in this unit. Then check your answers against the Answer Key which immediately follows the quiz questions.

1. Which of the following is a listing agent required to disclose?

   a. Title defects on the property
   b. The seller's criminal record
   c. The seller's HIV diagnosis
   d. Rumors that the property is haunted

2. Which form of agent representation is prohibited in Florida?

   a. Buyer agency
   b. Sister agency
   c. Dual agency
   d. Subagency

3. Sally listed a condo last week and has a buyer who wants to submit an offer. She is currently acting as a single agent to her sellers. What is the name of the brokerage relationship she will transition to when she starts representing both the buyer and seller in the transaction?

   a. She will be acting as a dual broker.
   b. She will be acting as a transaction broker.
   c. Sally will be a double agent.
   d. This transition is not allowed in Florida.

4. Which agency relationship consists of the sales associate working as the agent of a broker who is the agent of a buyer or seller?

   a. Broker agency
   b. Multiple agency
   c. Subagency
   d. Dual agency

5. Which of the following is an agent's duty to a customer?

   a. Skill
   b. Diligence
   c. Loyalty
   d. Fairness

6. Angela is working closely with an investor. The investor sends her a property and asks for her opinion. Angela is passionate about that particular neighborhood and insists that the value will appreciate significantly in the next few years, although she has no supporting data. Is what Angela said appropriate?

    a. Angela was negligent and misrepresented the facts on the property.
    b. Angela misrepresented her expertise. She can be held accountable if the property does not appreciate.
    c. She intentionally misrepresented the neighborhoods future.
    d. Angela is allowed to discuss the appreciation of properties.

===

Answer Key:

Unit Two: Brokerage Relationships and Licensee Disclosures

1. **a.** **Title defects on the property**
2. **c.** **Dual agency**
3. **b.** **She will be acting as a transaction broker.**
4. **c.** **Subagency**
5. **d.** **Fairness**
6. **b.** **Angela misrepresented her expertise. She can be held accountable if the property does not appreciate.**

===

UNIT 3:

BROKERAGE OPERATIONS REGULATION

Unit Three Learning Objectives: When the student has completed this unit he or she will be able to:

- Characterize salient regulations governing the operation of brokerage companies, including those relating to branches, escrow procedures, recordkeeping, and trade names.
- Describe the restrictions imposed on licensees as they conduct advertising activities and team-level marketing practices
- Characterize how regulations impact unlicensed assistants, working with rental lists, and collecting compensation for brokerage services

OFFICING, SIGNAGE, AND BRANCH LICENSING

Office requirements

Florida statute mandates that each active broker maintain an office that is located in a building of "stationary construction." The law further mandates that only brokers can own and maintain an office. Sales associates and broker associates may not have their own offices.

Brokers' offices must be registered with the Department of Business and Professional Regulation (DBPR). The office must include at least one enclosed room and have space to conduct private transactions. Additionally, the broker is required to keep any real estate files and records (physical or electronic) in the office so they are immediately available for inspection by the FREC or other governing authority.

If local zoning allows, the broker may set up the office in a residential location, such as the broker's home, as long as all office requirements are met, including display of the broker's sign.

Brance office registration

If a broker conducts business at a location other than the main office, the broker may be required to register the additional office as a branch office and pay the required registration fee for each such office. All branch offices must be registered.

Additionally, if the broker or brokerage's name or advertising is displayed on an office other than the main office in such a way as to lead the public to believe the office is owned or operated by that same broker, then that office must be registered as a branch office.

If a broker decides to close a branch office and open a new branch office at a different location, the broker must register the new office and pay the registration fee for that office. The registration for the closed branch office may not be transferred to the new branch office. If the broker decides to re-open the closed branch office within that office's license period, no additional fee will be required.

37

Office signage

Every office, whether main or branch, is required to display a sign at the entrance which can be seen and read easily by anyone entering the office. The sign can be on the exterior or interior entrance of the office. Florida law requires the sign to contain the broker's name and any trade name. If the brokerage is a partnership or corporation, the sign must contain the partnership or corporation's name or trade name as well as at least one of the brokers. The words "Licensed Real Estate Broker" or "Lic. Real Estate Broker" must be included on the entrance sign of any real estate brokerage or business entity.

Sales associate officing

Upon initial licensure, a sales associate must register with an employing broker in order to engage in practice. The sales associate must work under the direction, control, and management of the specified broker or an owner-developer. The associate must additionally work out of an office maintained by that same broker. The sales associate may be registered under only one broker at a time and may not operate as a broker or operate for any other broker who is not the associate's registered employing broker.

ADVERTISING REGULATIONS

Prohibitions

False or misleading advertising. Florida law prohibits licensees from placing or causing to be placed any advertisement for property or services that is fraudulent, false, deceptive, misleading, or exaggerated. This includes written ads as well as ads on television or radio that are used to induce the sale, purchase, or rental of real property.

Blind advertising. Florida law requires that all advertisements include the brokerage's licensed name so any reasonable person would know the ad is from a real estate licensee. The broker's nickname may be included in the advertising as long as his or her legal registered name is also included. The broker's personal name may also be included in the ad as long as the broker's last name as it is registered with the DBPR is included. Ads that do not include the brokerage's name are considered blind advertising and are prohibited.

Sales associates advertising or conducting business in own name. Brokerage services include advertising. Consequently, anyone placing advertisements must be a broker. Sales associates may create or place advertisements only under the supervision and in the name of their employing broker. Sales associates may not advertise in their own names. Any form of advertising created by a sales associate must include the brokerage's licensed name.

Unsupervised team advertising. Teams within a brokerage firm may advertise only under the supervision of the broker and in the name of the brokerage firm. Certain words, namely "brokerage," "realty," and the like, are not allowed as potentially creating confusion for the public. The name of the team must be in a font that is no larger than that used for the name or logo of the registered broker.

Misleading advertising identify. In addition to including the brokerage's name, real estate advertisements must be worded so that any reasonable person knows that the advertiser is a real estate licensee. They may not be worded in a way that makes the public believe the ad is from someone other than a real estate licensee.

Telephone Consumer Protection Act

The TCPA (Telephone Consumer Protection Act) addresses the regulation of unsolicited telemarketing phone calls. Rules include the following:

- Telephone solicitors are banned from using a pre-recorded voice to a residential line.
- Robocalls from telemarketers or debt collectors without prior express consumer consent are banned.
- Solicitors are banned from using an auto dialer to send text messages to cell phones without prior express consumer consent.
- Calls after 9 p.m. and before 8 a.m. in the consumer's time zone are banned
- telephone solicitors must identify themselves, on whose behalf they are calling, and how they can be contacted
- telemarketers must comply with any do-not-call request made during the solicitation call
- consumers can place their phone numbers on a national Do-Not-Call list which prohibits future solicitations from telemarketers.
- Robocalls must provide an automated opt-out function during the call.
- Consumers may sue companies that violate the law on a per-call basis.

CAN-SPAM Act

The CAN-SPAM Act supplements the Telephone Consumer Protection Act (TCPA) by covering solicitations through email. It

- bans sending unwanted email 'commercial messages' to wireless devices
- requires express prior authorization
- requires giving an 'opt out' choice to terminate the sender's messages

Florida state telemarketing laws

Florida telemarketing laws apply to businesses located within Florida and those outside the state who call Florida residents. The laws include the Florida Telemarketing Act and the Florida Telephonic Sales law. The laws include the following:

- Telephone solicitors must obtain a license from the Florida Division of Consumer Services before operating in Florida.
- Solicitors must restrict their calls to 8 a.m. to 9 p.m.
- Solicitors may not block caller ID.
- The solicitor has 30 seconds to state his or her true name, the name of the company the telemarketer represents, and the goods or services being sold.

Florida has its own do-not-call list that prohibits telemarketers from calling residential phones, cell phones, or paging devices. Additional information and the registry can be found online at https://www.fdacs.gov/Consumer-Resources/Florida-Do-Not-Call .

Real estate licensees are exempt when they are calling a property seller in response to a yard sign or other advertisement placed by the seller. However, a licensee is not exempt if the seller is a "for sale by owner" advertiser who has placed his or her telephone number on the national do-not-call list.

Team advertising

Team advertising occurs whenever one or more licensees use a name or logo to represent themselves to the public. FREC requires that such teams perform all activities under the supervision of the same broker or brokerage. Further, each team must designate a licensee to be responsible for all advertising compliance and maintaining an official roster of all team members.

Team names. Team names may include the terms "team" or "group," but may not include the following terms: Agency; Brokerage; Brokers; Company; Corporation; Corp.; Inc.; LLC; LP; LLP; Partnership; Property; Realty; or other term suggesting a separate entity. These restrictions apply to all advertising representations of a given team. In addition, the team name cannot appear in larger print that the name of the registered brokerage.

ESCROW REGULATIONS

Deposit regulations

An escrow, or trust, account is held by a third party to a transaction. It holds earnest money until the property ownership is transferred at closing. Title companies with trust powers and attorneys may also be used to hold funds in escrow.

Florida law mandates that the trust account hold only third-party funds with none of the licensee's personal funds intermingled. However, the law also allows the broker to deposit personal or brokerage funds into each escrow account to be used for account maintenance fees.

Sales associate funds delivery requirements. If a property buyer gives earnest money or any other deposit to a sales associate in relation to a real estate transaction, the sales associate is required to turn the funds over to his or her employing broker no later than the end of the next business day, not counting Saturdays, Sundays, or legal holidays.

Broker's trust fund deposit deadline. Florida administrative rules state that brokers who receive any form of transaction funds from their sales associates must "immediately" deposit those funds into an escrow account. The rule defines "immediately" as no later than the end of the third business day following receipt of the item to be deposited, excluding Saturdays, Sundays, and legal holidays.

The three business days begin when the sales associate receives the funds, not when the broker receives them from the sales associate.

Disputed escrow funds

FREC notification. When a real estate transaction does not close, the earnest money and any other related funds must be disbursed to the appropriate party. If the parties to the transaction do not agree on who should receive the funds, and both parties make demands for the funds, the broker must notify the FREC of the conflict within 15 business days of the last demand received for the funds. The broker

should use the Notice of Escrow Dispute/Good Faith Doubt form found online at
http://www.myfloridalicense.com/dbpr/re/documents/EDO_Notice.pdf .

Escrow Disbursement Order (EDO). An EDO is a determination made by the FREC as to who is entitled to the disputed escrow funds. If the funds are held by the broker, he or she can request the FREC issue an EDO. If the EDO is denied, then the broker must employ one of the other settlement procedures and notify the FREC of which procedure will be used. If the funds are held by an attorney or title company, the FREC will not issue an EDO.

Alternative settlement procedures

When the need arises to settle an escrow conflict or a good-faith doubt, the broker may use any of four settlement procedures, as follows.

Mediation. Mediation is an informal conflict settlement procedure that is conducted by a qualified third party. The intention of mediation is to bring the parties together with the guidance of the mediator and have the parties come to a mutually agreeable resolution. Mediation may be used to settle the conflict if all of the associated parties give written consent. Once an agreement is reached, it is put into writing and signed by both parties. It then becomes a binding contract. If the parties do not all consent to mediation or if the conflict is not settled in mediation within 90 days of the last demand, the broker must employ one of the other settlement procedures.

Arbitration. Arbitration is a process conducted by one or more third party arbitrators acting as judges. Typically, each side chooses one arbitrator, and then those two select a third. The arbitrators hear evidence, make decisions, and give written opinions. The arbitrators' decisions are binding. The conflicting parties must agree in writing to go to arbitration and must agree to comply with the arbitrators' final decision.

Litigation. Litigation a legal procedure either party may use if parties do not agree to mediation or arbitration. In this case, one party would file a lawsuit for the conflict to be heard in court to reach a resolution. However, because mediation is so successful and cost effective, Florida courts require most lawsuits to be mediated before a court will hear the case.

RECORDKEEPING, INSPECTIONS

Brokers must retain and maintain comprehensive records and documentation of all trust account activity including deposits, withdrawals, and statements. Further, the broker must make such trust records available to DBPR upon request.

Monthly reconciliations

Brokers must complete monthly trust account reconciliations. The reconciliations must reflect the broker's total trust liability (total of all deposits) being held. Each monthly reconciliation must be reviewed, signed and dated by the broker.

Document retention

Brokers must retain at least one legible copy of all accounts and records relating to the business for at least 5 years from the date of receipt of any monies or the execution of any transaction contracts.

Inspections and audits

All brokerages are subject to periodic regulatory office inspections and audits of records. The Department of Real Estate looks for regulatory compliance in the areas of officing, signage, relationship disclosures, licenses and escrow accounts. Specific points of inspection include the following:

Officing. Every active Florida broker must have a stationary office consisting of, at the minimum, one enclosed room where records are kept and negotiations are conducted.

Signage. The broker's office must have an official sign at the entrance of the facility. The sign must be readily visible to anyone entering the office. It must also contain the name of the brokerage firm (if any) and the name of the broker along with the words "licensed real estate broker."

Licenses and registration. Inspections will include an examination of all licensee's licenses and registration of the brokerage. These documents must be current and valid.

Agency disclosure. The inspection will look for documentation of the brokerage's agency policy and how disclosures are delivered. Here it is advisable to retain the actual disclosure documents utilized.

Escrow account audit. As indicated previously, brokers should expect a periodic escrow account audit. The audit will survey reconciliations, statements, lease agreements, canceled checks, receipts, bank activity and interest-bearing escrow agreements.

BUSINESS ENTITIY REGISTRATION

Entities that must register as brokers with DBPR

Sole proprietorship. A business or brokerage that is owned by one individual is called a sole proprietorship. A licensed broker may form a sole proprietorship by filing with the Florida Department of State (FDOS) and registering with the DBPR. The sole broker is responsible for all business and employee activities.

General partnership. Two or more individuals may form a general partnership and share in the business activities, finances, and profits of the partnership. The partnership must be registered with the DBPR. At least one partner must be a licensed broker, and all partners who deal with the public to perform real estate services must hold valid and current broker licenses.

Limited partnership. Limited partnerships are created by filing with the FDOS and must be registered with the DBPR. They must include at least one general partner, with all general partners required to register with the DBPR. At least one general partner must be a licensed broker. All general partners who deal with the public to perform real estate services also must be licensed brokers.

For profit corporation. To become a real estate brokerage, the corporation must register with the DBPR as a brokerage entity by submitting a brokerage corporation application. The corporation is required to have at least one of the officers or directors licensed as an active broker. The corporation may have licensed, unlicensed, and inactive brokers serve as officers or directors, but all who provide real estate services to the public must be licensed active brokers. The corporation must also register all unlicensed officers and directors for identification purposes.

Limited liability company (LLC). LLCs are separate and distinct legal entities wherein the owners are not personally liable for the entity's debts and liabilities. It allows owners to separate their business dealings from their personal affairs. Like other business entities, an LLC must be filed with the FDOS.

Sales associates and broker associates are prohibited from being officers, members, managers, or directors in a real estate brokerage corporation or a general partner in a brokerage limited or general partnership.

Entities not allowed to register

Business entities not allowed to register with DBPR include church organizations, joint ventures, business trusts, cooperative associations and unincorporated associations. Because they are unincorporated, they are not permitted to own property in their own name or to enter into contracts. Consequently, they may not register as a real estate broker.

TRADE NAMES

Brokers

Brokers register their brokerages under the broker's legal name or the business's legal name. They may also register under a trade name, a fictitious name other than their own name that the broker would like to use for the brokerage. The trade name must appear on the broker's license and registration and must be unique from any other business or trade name.

The broker may only register under one trade name and must have a new license issued if he or she changes the trade name. The registered trade name must appear on all brokerage signage and advertising.

Sales associates

Sales associates are not permitted to use a trade name or fictitious name. They must register under their real names and have only the real name show on the license.

Display of names. FREC administrative rules prohibit licensees from using or displaying any name, insignia, or designation of a real estate association or organization unless they are authorized to do so.

UNLICENSED ASSISTANTS; ALLOWED ACTIVITIES

Administrative assistants hired by licensees cannot perform real estate services without license. Moreover, it is Illegal to pay unlicensed assistants for performing real estate services.

Unlicensed assistants may provide ministerial support services. Specifically, they may

- submit listings to MLS

- assemble documents
- deposit trust monies
- compute commission checks
- place signs on properties
- prepare advertising for broker approval
- answer certain questions

COMMISSIONS

Prohibited practices

The following commission-related practices are prohibited in Florida.

Price fixing. When two or more brokers get together and agree to charge the same set commission percentage or fee for their services, this is called price fixing. Price fixing is against the law and leads to monopolies wherein competition is restricted. Antitrust laws encourage and protect competition and can impose criminal penalties on the price fixers. Each broker must establish his or her own commission rate separately from other brokers.

Sales associate contracting directly with principal. Sales associates work under the employment and supervision of a broker. They are prohibited from contracting directly with the principal or being paid directly by the principal. Any commission the sales associate receives must come directly from the employing broker based on the commission agreement the associate has with the broker and not directly from the principal.

Sales associate suing principal for commission. Because all contracts are between the principal and the broker, only the broker may sue a principal for unpaid commission. If the broker has been paid by the principal but does not pay the sales associate, the associate may sue the broker for the unpaid compensation but may not sue the principal directly.

Sharing a commission with an unlicensed person. Commissions are paid for services rendered in selling or purchasing property. Providing real estate services requires a real estate license. Therefore, only licensed real estate brokers and sales associates may provide such services. Consequently, sharing a commission with an unlicensed person is a violation of license law. The one exception allowed by the FREC is sharing the commission with a party to the transaction, such as the buyer or seller, as long as doing so is disclosed in writing to all parties to the transaction.

Paying an unlicensed person for performing real estate services. Again, providing real estate services requires a real estate license. Just as sharing a commission with an unlicensed person is prohibited, so is paying an unlicensed person to perform real estate services. Paying an unlicensed person for these services is a violation of license law.

Kickbacks and referral fees

Prohibition. Under the Real Estate Settlement Procedures Act (RESPA), it is illegal for a real estate licensee to accept a kickback or rebate from any business providing a service used to close a real estate transaction, such as a surveyor, appraiser, property inspector, title company, mortgage lender, etc. A kickback may take the form of favors, advertising, money, gifts, or other items of value given to the licensee or broker in return for sending clients to the particular service provider.

The licensee may utilize these service providers and pay them for services they actually perform. However, the licensee must not accept anything in return from the service provider for utilizing a particular provider.

The licensee also may not give or accept any portion, split, or percentage of any fee the service provider is paid for the service. Brokers may have affiliated business arrangements with certain service providers but must be careful that the arrangement does not include any illegal kickback or rebate.

Exceptions. Under certain conditions, kickbacks are legal, as follows:

- all parties to the transaction must be fully informed of the kickback
- the kickback must not be prohibited by any other law, such as RESPA
- a referral or finder's fee (no more than $50) may be paid to a tenant in an apartment complex for introducing a prospective tenant to the property management company or the complex owner for the purpose of renting or leasing an apartment
- as mentioned above, sharing a commission with an unlicensed buyer or seller as a rebate is allowed as long as all parties to the transaction are informed in writing
- a broker licensed in Florida may pay a referral fee or share a commission with a broker licensed or registered in a foreign state as long as the foreign broker does not violate any Florida law

Commission-related liens

Commercial brokers may place liens for unpaid commissions against an owner's net proceeds from the sale of commercial property. The lien, however, is against personal property, not against the real property transacted.

Residential brokers in Florida do not have lien rights for unpaid commissions against residential principals unless specifically authorized in the listing contract.

Construction lien law allows liens on real property for unpaid professional services, labor, or materials for property improvements and construction.

==

SNAPSHOT REVIEW: UNIT THREE

BROKERAGE OPERATIONS REGULATION

OFFICING, SIGNAGE, AND BRANCH LICENSING

Office requirements
- Active brokers must maintain an office in a building of "statutory construction"
- Only brokers can own and maintain an office
- Must be registered with the DBPR
- Must have at least one enclosed room and have space to conduct private transactions
- Broker must keep any real estate files and records in office

Branch office registration
- All branch offices must be registered
- Registration for a closed branch office may not be transferred to the new branch office

Office signage
- Sign must be displayed at office entrance; must contain broker's name and trade name with "Licensed Real Estate Broker" included; sales associates' names not required but must be below broker's name if included

Sales associate officing
- Sales associate must work under the direction, control, and management of the specified broker or an owner-developer

ADVERTISING REGULATIONS

Prohibitions
- False or misleading advertising; blind advertising; sales associate advertising or conducting business under own name

Telephone Consumer Protection Act
- No unsolicited calls, no robocalls, do not call compliance; opt-out option required; time of day restrictions
- Exemptions: nonprofits, political organizations, federal debt collectors, real estate licensee with buyer for "for sale by owner", with established business relationship, with business inquiry within last 3 months

CAN-SPAM Act

- No unsolicited email with commercial message and without prior consent

Florida state telemarketing laws
- Apply to businesses located within Florida and parties outside Florida calling Florida residents.
- Real estate licensees exempt when calling a property seller about a yard sign or other advertisement placed by the seller
- Licensee not exempt if seller is a "for sale by owner" advertiser with his/her telephone number on the national do-not-call list

- Florida Telemarketing Act and Florida Telephonic Sales law – solicitors need license; time of day restrictions; no blocking caller ID; payments not limited to credit cards; caller has 30 seconds to identify him/herself; provide right to cancel info

Team advertising

- Team advertising to be done under employing broker's supervision and name
- Team names may include the terms "team" or "group," but may not include the following terms: Agency; Brokerage; Brokers; Company; Corporation; Corp; Inc; LLC; LP; LLP; Partnership; Property; Realty; or other term suggesting a separate entity

ESCROW REGULATIONS

Deposit regulations

- Trust accounts can only hold third-party funds with none of the licensee's personal funds intermingled
- Sales associate receiving trust monies must give the funds to the broker no later than the end of the next business day, not counting Saturdays, Sundays, or legal holidays
- Brokers receiving transaction funds from sales associates must deposit funds into an escrow account within three business days, excluding Saturdays, Sundays, and legal holidays.

Disputed escrow funds

- If both parties make demands for the escrow funds, the broker must notify the FREC of the conflict within 15 business days. The broker should use the Notice of Escrow Dispute/Good Faith Doubt form found online
- If the funds are held by the broker, he or she can request that FREC issue an Escrow Disbursement Order

Alternative settlement procedures

- When the need arises to settle an escrow conflict, broker may employ settlement procedures of mediation, arbitration, or litigation

RECORDKEEPING, INSPECTIONS

- The broker must keep files and transaction records in the office; must be immediately available for inspection by the FREC; must keep records for at least 5 years

Monthly reconciliations

- The reconciliations must reflect the broker's total trust liability (total of all deposits) being held

Document retention

- Brokers must retain at least one copy of all accounts and records relating to the business for at least 5 years from the date of receipt of any monies or the execution of any transaction contracts

Inspections and audits

- Specific points of inspection include the following: officing, signage, licenses and registration, agency disclosure, and escrow account audit

BUSINESS ENTITY REGISTRATION

- Brokers register their brokerages under the broker's legal name or the business's legal name

Entities that must register as brokers with DBPR

- Sole proprietorship; general partnership; limited partnership; for profit corporation; LLC

Entities not allowed to register
- Church organizations; joint ventures; business trusts; cooperative associations; unincorporated associations

TRADE NAMES

- Fictitious name used as business name; must be registered and appear on license, signage, advertising
- Sales associates prohibited from using trade name
- Licensee must be authorized to display name, insignia, or designation of an association

Brokers
- The trade name must appear on the broker's license and registration, and all brokerage signage and advertising. It must be unique from any other business or trade name
- The broker may only register under one trade name and must have a new license issued if he or she changes the trade name

Sales associates
- Sales associates are not permitted to use a trade name or fictitious name. They must register under their real names and have only the real name show on the license

UNLICENSED ASSISTANTS; ALLOWED ACTIVITIES

- Unlicensed assistants may submit listings to MLS, assemble documents, deposit trust monies, compute commission checks, place signs on properties, prepare advertising for broker approval, and answer certain questions

COMMISSIONS

Prohibited practices
- Price fixing; sales associate contracting directly with principal; sales associate suing principal for commission; sharing commission with an unlicensed person; paying unlicensed person for performing real estate services

Kickbacks and referral fees
- Prohibited: acceptance of favors, advertising, money, gifts, etc. for referring clients to certain businesses unless all parties are informed, paying referral fee to tenant, sharing commission with foreign broker
- A licensed broker may pay a referral fee or share a commission with a broker licensed or registered in a foreign state

Commission-related liens
- Commercial brokers may place liens for unpaid commissions against an owner's net proceeds from the sale of commercial property; does not apply to residential transactions

==

Check Your Understanding Quiz:

Unit Three: Brokerage Operations Regulation

Carefully read each question then provide your best answer based on what you learned in this unit. Then check your answers against the Answer Key which immediately follows the quiz questions.

1. Brokers Abigail and Joseph are preparing for a listing appointment with the same seller. Before parting ways, they both agree to ask for a 6% commission and refuse to negotiate. What are they participating in?

   a. Cost freezing
   b. Price fixing
   c. Listing monopoly
   d. Commission solidarity

2. Sam the surveyor is trying to get more business so he starts offering real estate agents $100 per referred client. What should the real estate agents do?

   a. They should accept the money.
   b. Real estate licensees cannot accept givebacks.
   c. They should ask for a higher referral payment.
   d. Since it is a kickback, it is illegal for agents to accept it.

3. Which statute bans prerecorded calls without prior consumer consent?

   a. The Robocall Protection Act
   b. The Phone Soliciting Act
   c. The Telephone Consumer Protection Act
   d. The Do Not Call Statute

4. Are advertisements without the brokerage's name allowed?

   a. These types of advertisements are allowed, as long as the licensee's name is included.
   b. This is called blind advertising and it is prohibited.
   c. This is brokerage neglect and it is illegal.
   d. This is called licensee manipulation and it is not allowed.

5. Florida law mandates that escrow accounts do not hold any _____.

   a. rental property deposits.
   b. earnest money deposits.
   c. rent payments.
   d. licensee personal funds.

6. Which of the following is an appropriate real estate team name?

    a. Miami Luxury Realty
    b. Orlando Key Brokerage
    c. Tampa Home Sweet Home Team
    d. Welcome Home Agency

==

Answer Key:

Unit Three: Brokerage Relationships and Licensee Disclosures

1. **b. Price fixing**
2. **d. Since it is a kickback, it is illegal for agents to accept it.**
3. **c. The Telephone Consumer Protection Act**
4. **b. This is called blind advertising and it is prohibited.**
5. **d. licensee personal funds.**
6. **c. Tampa Home Sweet Home Team**

SECTION TWO:
BUSINESS ETHICS & PRACTICES

UNITS 4-6

Unit 4: **Professional Practices & Realtors® Code of Ethics, Part I**

Unit 5: **Realtors® Code of Ethics, Part II**

Unit 6: **Realtors® Code of Ethics, Part III**

UNIT 4:

PROFESSIONAL PRACTICES AND REALTORS® CODE OF ETHICS, PART I

Unit Four Learning Objectives: When the student has completed this unit he or she will be able to:

- Summarize the role, general structure and organization of the Realtor® Code of Ethics.
- Describe the purpose and import of the Preamble for the Code of Ethics
- Characterize the general import and practical applicability of Articles 1-9 of the Realtors® Code of Ethics

DEFINITIONS

Business ethics

The standards used by a business or company to make decisions and how they treat their Clients, Customers, Vendors, and Employees.

Client

An individual in which we have a fiduciary relationship, such as a Single Agency Relationship.

Code of Ethics

A set of rules and conduct members must practice in their dealings with others. These standards lay out the values of an organization.

Customer

An individual with whom we do not have a fiduciary relationship and owe limited disclosure, such as a Transaction Brokerage Relationship.

Ethics

A system of moral principles, rules, an individual or business uses to determine how they deal with others.

Morals

A person's individuals belief of what is right and wrong; religion, culture, and many other factors influence a person's morals.

Preamble

The opening statement of a document reflecting the values or vision of the organization.

Situational Ethics

A person changing their ethical views to fit a specific situation or changing how they react due to a change in circumstance.

BUSINESS ETHICS: AN OVERVIEW

If you ever decided to get an MBA, it will come to understand the term **business ethics**. Every MBA program in the United States is required to offer at least one course in business ethics. This requirement shows the environment that we operate within our society today.

We have seen scandals in recent years involving companies breaking some fundamental ethical and legal practices. In the United States, scandals such as the Martha Stewart insider-trading, controversy over elections, the security of the election process, Enron and Arthur Anderson, and the College Admission Scandal, to name a few, identify some of the lapses in Business Ethics in our country. These scandals have significantly affected our country and reinforced our need to watch our businesses and ethics system. It is essential to understand the difference between ethics and morals and how we acquire each.

Morals

Morals are our individual beliefs and the belief system in which we live. Our morals come from our parents, the culture we live in, and our religious upbringing. For many, the foundation of morals is the Golden Rule. It is the guidance we should all live our lives by, "Do unto others as you would have done unto you."

Ethics

Ethics are the rules by which we live of lives. In the book, "Is It Still Cheating If I Don't Get Caught?", Bruce Weinstein identified five principles of ethics that are the same in all religions:

- Do no harm
- Make things better
- Respect others
- Be fair
- Be loving

Variability of ethics. Ethics can change from culture to culture. For example, in the United States, a business would never think to budget money to pay for the safe return of kidnapped executives or employees or pay a bribe to government officials. Companies operating in this manner would find themselves in legal trouble, along with violating our country's ethics systems.

However, in other countries, it is common to pay government officials to get work done or get permits to operate within a specific region. In some South American countries, US companies must budget into projects protect for their executives and employees. They must budge to pay ransom demands or provide personnel with hostage insurance policies.

Good morals would tell us how to act in this situation; however, ethics is different in each country, religion, and culture. In some parts of the world, this activity is just part of doing business, and you plan for it and budget for it as part of your day-to-day operations.

Situational ethics

The preceding is an example of what is called **situational ethics**. Everyone practices situational ethics to some degree or another. Situational ethics are individuals looking at the circumstances around them and making a behavioral decision based on a sequence of events and not on the events as they would play out to society. In the earlier example, the business must approach similar projects differently depending on where they are operating. In the United States, bribing government officials to get work done or something overlooked is unethical. It would also be illegal in many cases, but this practice is common in other countries. Companies must decide if they are willing to do these things or not work in that part of the world.

Situational ethics illustrated. Consider two illustrations of situational ethics. What would your answers be to the questions posed?

- Example 1: You are a college real estate student and have an exam tonight; however, you did not get to study as you wanted. You know the girl who sits beside you in class is very smart, so you decide to copy her answers during the test. Is this ethical? Is this legal? Is it moral?

- Example 2: You are taking an online real estate class. During an exam, you cannot remember the meaning of a specific term. No one is watching you, and your book is right next to you. You open the book and look up the word and then continue to your next question. Is this ethical? Is this legal? Is it moral?

What is the difference between the two scenarios?

NAR'S CODE OF ETHICS

Historical abstract

In the early 1900s, real estate agents were given licenses by county judges, and often they were "peddlers" licenses. The 1900s was a time of land scams and speculation. In 1908, the National

Association of Realtors® (NAR) formed to eliminate the notion of "Caveat emptor" or let the buyer beware. Their goal was to protect the public and promote homeownership in the United States.

In 1913, NAR introduced the Code of Ethics for Realtors® to follow in their dealings with their clients, the public, and other Realtors®. This document has been fluid and ever-changing over the years. Today, Realtors® have one of the strongest professional Code of Ethics in the United States.

The Code of Ethics also provides standard practices and procedures setting forth how Realtors® should react in their dealings with specific individuals and others in their field. The Code of Ethics, however, is not law. Rather, the Code of Ethics enhances local, state, or federal laws.

A quote in the 2020/2021 Code of Ethics and Arbitration Manual reads, "Because the Code is a living document and real estate is a dynamic business and profession, the law need never be its substitute. So long as the aspiration to better serve the public remails the underlying concept of the code, it must evolve and grow in significance and importance consonant with but independent of the law."

Structure of the Code of Ethics

The Code of Ethics has four parts:

- The Preamble
- Duties to Clients and Customers (Articles 1 – 9)
- Duties to the Public (Articles 10 – 14)
- Duties to Realtors® (Articles 15 – 17)

The Articles within the Code of Ethics define the broad statements about the licensee's behavior and duties. The **Standards of Practice**, within each Article, gives more specific guidance to the licensee. The Standards of Practice support and interpret the Articles.

In resolving ethics complaints, complainants are to cite only the Article(s) violated and not the Standard of Practice. It will be up to the Professional Standards Committee to give the specific Standard of Practice violated in their final report.

PREAMBLE

"Under all is the land."

This statement is a powerful start to NAR's Code of Ethics. It means that everything we do, are, or aspire to become, begins with the land beneath our feet. The quote shows the importance of the role each Realtor® holds in our society. Real estate impacts everything.

The Preamble of the Code of Ethics serves as a vision statement on how licensees should conduct themselves and represent their profession to the public. The Preamble calls for Realtors® to "maintain and improve the standards of their calling." It also states that it is the Realtor's responsibility to "act with integrity and honesty."

As of January 1, 2021, the Board of Directors of NAR changed the Preamble. It added that licensees should not dishonor the profession or do anything that will hurt the organization's public trust. The Board of Directors altered the Preamble wording to reflect the changes in Article 10 of the Code of Ethics (see also Chapter 5).

SECTION 1 – DUTIES TO CLIENTS AND CUSTOMERS

ARTICLE 1

> "When representing a buyer, seller, landlord, tenant, or other client as an agent, REALTORS® pledge themselves to protect and promote the interests of their client. This obligation to the client is primary, but it does not relieve REALTORS® of their obligation to treat all parties honestly. When serving a buyer, seller, landlord, tenant or other party in a non-agency capacity, REALTORS® remain obligated to treat all parties honestly."

Central themes. Article 1 of the Code of Ethics promotes honesty as a critical virtue of any licensee. The 16 Standards of Practices within Article 1 describes the different duties a licensee may have and how they must act in specific situations. The basis of the Standards of Practices is the duties owed to our customers and clients based on Florida's Agency Law.

Article 1 Standards of Practice. The central thrust of Article 1 is reflected in its Standards of Practices 1.1 through 1.16. These are as follows:

SP 1.1 – Be careful to abide by the Code when you are representing yourself in a transaction.
SP 1.2 – The Code of Ethics applies to all transactions.
SP 1.3 – Do not mislead the owner as to the real market value of a piece of property.
SP 1.4 – Do not mislead the savings or benefits of utilizing the services of a Realtor®.
SP 1.5 – No dual agency. An agent cannot have a fiduciary relationship with both parties in a transaction.
SP 1.6 – Submit all offers and counteroffers promptly.
SP 1.7 – When working as the listing agent, present all offers until closing, unless waived in writing.
SP 1.8 – When working as the buyer's agent, present all offers until contract acceptance, unless waived in writing.
SP 1.9 – Maintain confidentiality even after termination of a relationship.
SP 1.10 – In property management, the licensee must comply with the management agreement and ensure their tenants' rights, safety, and health.
SP 1.11 – Use skill, care, and diligence in all transactions.

SP 1.12 - Disclose to sellers and landlords cooperation policy and compensation to all parties.

SP 1.13 – Disclose cooperation with other brokers.

SP 1.14 – Appraisal fees must not be based on the market value of the property.

SP 1.15 – Disclose any other offers already presented or any expected offers.

SP 1.16 – Do not enter the property without permission or authorization from the owner.

Article 1 illustration. A broker was preparing a CMA for a listing appointment. The broker knew the seller was interviewing several other brokers. He decided to increase the property's market value to show the seller how much more money they could earn from hiring him. The violation in this example is of Article 1, Standard Practice 1.3 and 1.4.

ARTICLE 2

"REALTORS® shall avoid exaggeration, misrepresentation, or concealment of pertinent facts relating to the property or the transaction. REALTORS® shall not, however, be obligated to discover latent defects in the property, to advise on matters outside the scope of their real estate license, or to disclose facts which are confidential under the scope of agency or non-agency relationships as defined by state law."

Central theme. Article 2 of the Code of Ethics discusses the need for transparency in all transactions. While a licensee is not required to seek out defects in the property, they must disclose any defects they know exists. This duty is necessary no matter the type of agency relationship the broker has established.

Article 2 Standards of Practice. Article 2 has five Standards of Practice:

SP 2.1 – A Realtor® must disclose any latent defects they know about or that are readily observable to a lay-person. They are not required to be experts in fields other than their own.

SP 2.2 – Moved to Standard of Practice 1.12

SP 2.3 – Moved to Standard of Practice 1.13

SP 2.4 – A Realtor® must not participate in doctoring the numbers on any contract.

SP 2.5 – Realtors® must not disclose non-material items not pertinent to the transaction.

Article 2 illustration. Susie is showing a potential buyer a house. The MLS stated that the roof was 25 years old and had a few leaks. During the showing, Susie's customer asked about the condition of the roof. Susie stated she was not aware of any problems. Susie has violated Article 2, Standard 2.1.

ARTICLE 3

> *"REALTORS® shall cooperate with other brokers except when cooperation is not in the client's best interest. The obligation to cooperate does not include the obligation to share commissions, fees, or to otherwise compensate another broker."*

Central theme. Article 3 promotes cooperation among brokers unless it is not in their client's best interest.

Article 3 Standards of Practice. Article 3 has eleven Standards of Practice as follows:

SP 3.1 – Realtors® must establish terms of cooperation.

SP 3.2 - Realtors® who change the compensation in a transaction must communicate it to other licensees.

SP 3.3 – Realtors® may change the cooperative compensation.

SP 3.4 – Realtors® must disclose variable rate commissions.

SP 3.5 – Realtors® must disclose all pertinent facts before and after the sale.

SP 3.6 - Realtors® should disclose any current accepted offers.

SP 3.7 – Realtors® must disclose their status when calling other Realtors® about a listed property.

SP 3.8 – Realtors® must not give false information about the availability of property to be shown.

SP 3.9 – Realtors® must not provide access to a listed property in any way other than what is agreed upon by the seller.

SP 3.10 – Realtor should share information on listed property and make the property available to other brokers.

SP 3.11 – Realtors® may not violate Fair Housing laws and refuse to show a piece of property to someone in a protected class.

Article 3 illustration. Janet's seller told her that they did not want to sell their home to anyone who was not white. Janet told potential buyers who were not white that the house was no longer available or was not available to be shown. The violation in this example is of Article 3, Standards of Practice 3.8 and 3.11.

ARTICLE 4

> *"REALTORS® shall not acquire an interest in or buy or present offers from themselves, any member of their immediate families, their firms, or any member thereof, or any entities in which they have any ownership interest, any real property without making their true position known to the owner or the owner's agent or broker. In selling property, they own, or in which they have any interest, REALTORS® shall reveal their ownership or interest in writing to the purchaser or the purchaser's representative."*

Central theme. Article 4 requires Realtors® to disclose that they have a real estate license when buying or selling property for themselves. If they do not disclose this fact, then they have an unfair advantage over the average consumer. By telling them, the Realtor® is giving them a chance to obtain representation in the transaction. Thus, keeping it an arms-length transaction.

Article 4 Standard of Practice. The one Standard of Practice for Article 4 requires the Realtor® to reveal their ownership or interest in the property in writing before entering into any contract.

ARTICLE 5

"REALTORS® shall not undertake to provide professional services concerning a property or its value where they have a present or contemplated interest unless such interest is specifically disclosed to all affected parties."

Central theme. Article 5 requires Realtors® to disclose any conflict of interest before providing any professional services. The only time this would be allowed is with the written permission of all parties involved in providing the service.

Article 5 illustration. ABC Realty shares office space with a lender and a title company. They recommend that all their buyers use these companies since they are in the same location, and it allows them to communicate with the lender and title company to ensure the closing goes smoothly. What the Realtor® did not disclose to their customers is the fact that family members own these companies.

ARTICLE 6

"REALTORS® shall not accept any commission, rebate, or profit on expenditures made for their client, without the client's knowledge and consent.

When recommending real estate products or services (e.g., homeowner's insurance, warranty programs, mortgage financing, title insurance, etc.), REALTORS® shall disclose to the client or customer to whom the recommendation is made any financial benefits or fees, other than real estate referral fees, the REALTOR® or REALTOR®'s firm may receive as a direct result of such recommendation."

Central theme. Article 6 states a Realtor® may not accept any compensation in the form of a commission, rebate, kickback, etc., without the client's written consent. This requirement includes gifts from home inspectors, appliance companies, plumbers, etc.

Article 6 illustrated. A Realtor® hired Ace Home Inspection to inspect a home for a buyer. The Realtor did not tell the buyer that he received a $50 gift card for the referral. The Realtor® violates Article 6 of the Code of Ethics.

ARTICLE 7

> *"In a transaction, REALTORS® shall not accept compensation from more than one party, even if permitted by law, without disclosure to all parties and the informed consent of the REALTOR®'s client or clients."*

Central theme. Article 7 states that a Realtor® cannot accept compensation from more than one person without disclosing the fact to all parties. The Realtor should also have that consent in writing.

Article 7 illustrated. A broker has a Buyer's Broker Agreement with a buyer. The agreement states that the broker will get a 3% commission on a home valued at $350,000. The broker finds a home for $300,000 that the buyer likes, and they enter a contract. The broker is getting 3% from the listing broker and then asks the buyer to pay him a 3% commission. The broker tells the buyer he is not getting any commission from the seller's side. This type of action would be a violation of Article 7 of the Code of Conduct. The broker may not receive compensation from more than one party in a transaction unless he has written all the parties' written consent.

ARTICLE 8

> *"REALTORS® shall keep in a special account in an appropriate financial institution, separated from their own funds, monies coming into their possession in trust for other persons, such as escrows, trust funds, clients' monies, and other like items."*

Article 8 central themes. Article 8 addresses escrow funds and how to handle other people's money. A Broker must be careful not to commingle funds. Commingle is mixing their personal money with money held in trust for others. The only time commingling is legal is when a Broker puts up to $1,000 of personal funds for a Sales Escrow Account or $5,000 in a Tenant Escrow Account to stop the possibility of conversion.

ARTICLE 9

> *"REALTORS®, for the protection of all parties, shall assure whenever possible that all agreements related to real estate transactions including, but not limited to, listing and representation agreements, purchase contracts, and leases are in writing in clear and understandable language expressing the specific terms, conditions, obligations, and commitments of the parties. A copy of each agreement shall be furnished to each party to such agreements upon their signing or initialing."*

Central themes. Article 9 states Brokers must ensure all documents related to a real estate transaction be in clear, concise language. The contracts must also clearly represent the terms and conditions of the agreement between the parties. Florida law requires that the broker keep all contracts and real estate related transaction documents for five years or two years after the end of any litigation.

Article 9 Standards of Practice. Article 9 has 2 Standards of Practice as follows:

SP 9.1 – Realtors® should use reasonable care to ensure extensions and amendments.

SP 9.2 – Realtors® should make a reasonable effort to explain the different parts of a contract to clients when working electronically.

Article 9 illustrated. Broker Jane is working with a buyer in another state. She sends them an electronic contract and indicates where the buyer needs to sign. Jane does not review the Sales and Purchase Agreement with them or go over any of the disclosures. Upon return of the contract, Jane does not send a copy to the buyer. Broker Jane violates Article 9 of the Code of Articles.

===

SNAPSHOT REVIEW: UNIT FOUR

PROFESSIONAL PRACTICES AND REALTORS® CODE OF ETHICS, PART I

BUSINESS ETHICS

- Business ethics is now an important topic due to recent trends in malpractice; business ethics is a set of standards by which a company operates.

Morals

- a belief system put together as individuals mature and are influenced by our culture and religion.

Situational ethics

- decisions based on current circumstances versus how they affect the individual rather than how they affect society.

NAR'S CODE OF ETHICS

- was established in 1913. Its primary goal is to protect the public from land scams and to promote homeownership.

Structure of the Code of Ethics

- The Code of Ethics has four parts: The Preamble, Duties to Clients and Customers, Duties to the Public, and Duties to Realtors.

PREAMBLE

- of the Code of Ethics serves as a vision statement and lays out the duties and responsibilities for Realtors®.

SECTION 1: DUTIES TO CLIENTS AND CUSTOMERS

- covers the first 9 Articles
- Standards of practices are more detailed requirements of each Article within the Code of Ethics.

ARTICLE 1

- promotes honesty to all.

ARTICLE 2

- Realtor's® actions must have transparency to them.

ARTICLE 3

- promotes cooperation among brokers unless it is not in their client's best interest.

ARTICLE 4

- Realtors® must disclose that they have a real estate license when buying, selling, or renting their own property.

ARTICLE 5

- Realtors® must disclose any conflict of interest before providing professional services.

ARTICLE 6

- Realtors® may not accept any compensation without the written consent of all parties.

ARTICLE 7

- Realtors may not accept compensation from more than one person without disclosing the fact to all parties.

ARTICLE 8

- addresses the handling of escrow funds.

ARTICLE 9

- states that all documents must be in clear and concise language.

===

Check Your Understanding Quiz:

Unit Four: Professional Practices and Realtors® Code Of Ethics, Part I

Carefully read each question then provide your best answer based on what you learned in this unit. Then check your answers against the Answer Key which immediately follows the quiz questions.

1. Which of the following is considered to be ethical behavior?

    a. Cheating on a school exam
    b. Taking credit for your colleague's work
    c. Discriminating against a client due to their race
    d. Disclosing all the defects of a home you are selling

2. The Articles of the NAR Code of Ethics deal with all the following duties, EXCEPT

    a. Duties to your neighbors
    b. Duties to clients and customers
    c. Duties to the public
    d. Duties to other Realtors®

3. When was the Code of Ethics introduced?

    a. 1908
    b. 1964
    c. 1913
    d. 2021

4. The central theme of Article 1 of the NAR Code of Ethics is

    a. deal honestly with everyone no matter what type of relationship.
    b. disclose all defects of a home you are selling.
    c. use skill, care, and diligence if working with exclusive clients.
    d. do not violate fair housing laws.

5. You know that it is illegal and unethical to buy shares of a company you represent and receive information not available to the public. However, you have invested your children's college fund in the stock of your husband's company. Your husband tells you the company is about to go through an IRS audit, and he is worried about the outcome.

    The next morning you call your stockbroker to protect your children's college fund and ask him to sell all your stock and reinvest it in another company. This is an example of

a.   business ethics
b.   situational ethics
c.   Code of Ethics
d.   morals

6.   A broker is selling his home as a For Sale by Owner. A potential buyer comes to look at the house, and the broker shows him around. The buyer puts in a 95% offer, and the seller accepts it. After closing, the buyer finds out the seller is a real estate broker and never disclosed it. Has this broker violated the Code of Ethics, and if so, why?.

a.   No, since the buyer is only a customer
b.   No, since the offer was ultimately accepted
c.   Yes, since one must disclose his or her licensed status according to Article 4
d.   Yes, since the property was a For Sale by Owner

===

Answer Key:

Unit Four: Professional Practices and REALTORS® CODE OF ETHICS, PART I

1.   d. Disclosing all the defects of a home you are selling.

2.   a. Duties to your neighbors.

3.   c. 1913

4.   a. Deal honestly with everyone no matter what type of relationship.

5.   b. Situational Ethics

6.   c. Yes, since one must disclose his or her licensed status according to Article 4

Interactive Exercises

Unit 4: Professional Practices and Realtors® Code Of Ethics, Part I

SITUATIONAL CASE STUDY:

Agent John showed Broker Eric's listing to buyer clients, Adam and Eve. The list price in the MLS was $210,000. John contacted Eric to inquire about any offers on the property. Eric told John he had no offers. John then prepared an offer to submit to Eric.

Eric did have an offer for $185,000 cash from Jill and Jack. The seller accepted the offer, not knowing that John's clients submitted a bid for $205,000 with FHA financing and a 5% down payment.

Once John had submitted the offer, he asked Eric for written confirmation that the offer was presented to the seller. Eric never presented the offer, nor were Adam and Eve advised that there was another offer.

When asked, Eric stated that the seller had rejected the offer for a cash deal. Eric decided not to present the offer to the seller because it involved financing and would take longer to close. Eric wanted it to close before the end of the month to win an office selling contest.

DISCUSSION QUESTIONS:

1. How would you have handled the offers if you were Eric?

2. What Articles of the Code of Ethics do you feel were violated?

3. What specific Standards of Practices do you feel were violated?

CASE DEBRIEF:

1. Eric should have presented both offers. He then should have explained the pros and cons of each offer. The final decision is up to the sellers on whom they want to buy their house.

2. In this situation, the Professional Standards board determined that Eric violated Articles 1 and 3 of the NAR Code of Ethics.

3. The Standards of Practices violated are:
   SP 1.6 – Submit all offers and counteroffers objectively and as quickly as possible.
   SP 1.7 – The listing brokers must continue to submit offers they receive up to closing.
   SP 1.15 – When asked by the cooperating broker, the listing broker should disclose that he has other offers.
   SP 3.6 – The Realtor® should reveal the existence of accepted offers.

UNIT 5:

REALTORS® CODE OF ETHICS, PART II

Unit Five Learning Objectives: When the student has completed this unit he or she will be able to:

- Identify the protected classes from Article 10.
- Explain the duties a Realtor® owes to the public.
- Summarize the changes in Article 10 and give examples of violations.
- Identify common errors in advertising made by Realtors®.

DEFINITIONS

Demographic information

Information gathered on customers or clients. May include information such as age, sex, race, color, or national origin. This information is collected only to assist in operating the brokerage and identifying advertising avenues, not discriminating against anyone in a protected class.

Professional services

The eight professional services a Realtor® may perform are advertising, buying, auctioning, renting, selling, appraising, leasing, and exchanging.

NAR's protected classes

The NAR Code of Ethics' protected classes includes race, color, religion, sex, handicap, familial status, national origin, sexual orientation, or gender identity.

Public trust

Public Trust refers to misappropriation of client or customer funds or property, discrimination against the protected classes under the Code of Ethics, or fraud.

Duties to the public

The third section of NAR's Code of Ethics covers how Realtors® should behave when interacting with the public. Articles 10 to 14 and their Standards of Practices identify specific behavior and guidelines for dealing with the public. This section restates many of the same ideas expressed in Articles 1 through 9; however, it explicitly identifies the duties owed to the member of the public.

67

ARTICLE 10

"REALTORS® shall not deny equal professional services to any person for reasons of race, color, religion, sex, handicap, familial status, national origin, sexual orientation, or gender identity. REALTORS® shall not be parties to any plan or agreement to discriminate against a person or persons on the basis of race, color, religion, sex, handicap, familial status, national origin, sexual orientation, or gender identity."

"REALTORS®, in their real estate employment practices, shall not discriminate against any person or persons on the basis of race, color, religion, sex, handicap, familial status, national origin, sexual orientation, or gender identity."

Central theme. Article 10 of the Code of Ethics prohibits Realtors® from discrimination against the protected classes identified in the Code of Ethics. NAR has added protected classes to their Code of Ethics, making it stricter than the Federal Fair Housing Laws and the State of Florida's Fair Housing Laws.

Article 10 Standards of Practice. Article 10 has 5 Standards of Practices as follows:

SP 10.1 – Realtors® may provide necessary demographic information of a neighborhood; however, they cannot provide information about the neighborhood's racial, religious, or ethnic composition.

SP 10.2 – Realtors® may gather demographic information; however, they must be careful how the information is used and distributed.

SP 10.3 – Realtors® should be cautious with any advertisement that indicates a neighborhood's racial or ethnic makeup or targets one of the protected classes.

SP 10.4 – Realtors® must follow fair employment practices of employees or independent contractors.

SP 10.5 – Realtors® may not use harassing speech, hate speech, epithets, or slurs against someone in one of the protected classes.

Amendments to SP 10.5. In November 2020, the NAR Board of Directors made changes to Standard Practice 10.5. After extensive research, the Professional Standards Committee recommended changes that effectively broadened the context of this standard. In the past, the Code of Ethics only covered Realtors'® activities during a real estate transaction. The applicability of the new Standard of Practice 10.5 covers all activities of a Realtor.®

Under the changes made in November 2020, a Realtor® can be found guilty of a Code of Ethics violation whether the infraction related to a transaction, or other membership-related context. Presently, any potential breach of Article will be looked at individually to see if it is in violation of Article 10 or if it is someone expressing their First Amendment rights.

The new wording of Article 10, SP 10.5 became:
"Realtors® must not use harassing speech, hate speech, epithets, or slurs" based upon an individual or group that falls under one of the protected classes."

Article 10 illustration. A Realtor® created an advertisement using models and demographic information about a neighborhood's racial makeup. The purpose was primarily to steer specific individuals to a particular community. This action is a violation of Article 10, Standards of Practice 10.2 and 10.3.

ARTICLE 11

"The services which REALTORS® provide to their clients and customers shall conform to the standards of practice and competence which are reasonably expected in the specific real estate disciplines in which they engage; specifically, residential real estate brokerage, real property management, commercial and industrial real estate brokerage, land brokerage, real estate appraisal, real estate counseling, real estate syndication, real estate auction, and international real estate."

"REALTORS® shall not undertake to provide specialized professional services concerning a type of property or service that is outside their field of competence unless they engage the assistance of one who is competent on such types of property or service, or unless the facts are fully disclosed to the client. Any persons engaged to provide such assistance shall be so identified to the client, and their contribution to the assignment should be set forth."

Central theme. Realtors® should only work within real estate areas in which they have sufficient knowledge to protect their customer or client. One agent can't know everything about all areas of specialization within the industry.

Article 11 Standards of Practice. Article 11 has four Standards of Practice as follows:

SP 11.1 – When preparing an opinion of value on a piece of property, they must know that specific area of real estate and provide detailed information to the customer or client.

SP 11.2 – A Realtor® should perform only in an area that they have reasonable competence.

SP 11.3 – When providing consulting services or advice, they shall objectively present the material. The fee shall be contingent on the level of difficulty and the market value of the real property.

SP 11.4 – Competency required under Article 11 is based on the services agreed to by the customers or clients and follows the Code of Ethics and state law.

Article 11 illustration. A Realtor® is asked to prepare an appraisal for a bank on a commercial building's short sale. The agent had no experience in doing an appraisal or in commercial real estate. This agent would be guilty of violating Article 11 Standards of Practice 11.1, 11.2, and 11.4.

ARTICLE 12

"REALTORS® shall be honest and truthful in their real estate communications and shall present a true picture in their advertising, marketing, and other representations. REALTORS® shall ensure that their status as real estate professionals is readily apparent in their advertising, marketing, and other representations and that the recipients of all real estate communications are, or have been, notified that those communications are from a real estate professional."

Central theme. Realtors® should be honest in all their advertising and marketing.

Article 12 Standards of Practice. Article 12 has 13 Standards of Practices:

SP 12.1 – Realtors® who advertise something as free must disclose if they will receive any compensation and from whom they are going to receive the payment.

SP 12.2 – Deleted in January 2020.

SP 12.3 – Realtors® should use care if offering a prize or other compensation for real estate services. They must fully disclose the requirement to receive the compensation.

SP 12.4 – Realtors® should not advertise a property they are not authorized to market.

SP 12.5 – Realtors® must be careful not to practice Blind Advertising. The brokerage name must always appear in all advertising.

SP 12.6 – When selling their own property, a Realtor® must disclose their license status.

SP 12.7 – Only the brokers directly involved in a transaction may advertise that they sold or have a contract on the property with permission from the owner.

SP 12.8 – A Realtors® website should present current, accurate information, and they should keep the information current.

SP 12.9 – A Realtors® website shall disclose the brokerage's name and licensure state in a readily apparent manner.

SP 12.10 – Realtors® must advertise truthfully and give correct information and not deceptive the public in their URLs, websites, or the images they use.

SP 12.11 – Realtors® who intend to sell consumer information should disclose this wherever they gather the data.

SP 12.12 – Realtors® shall not use URL or domain names that may mislead the public.

SP 12.13 - Realtors® are only allowed to use designations, certifications, and other credentials they have earned and have maintained membership.

Article 12 illustration.

A Realtor® developed a website in which he promoted himself as the top producing agent in his area. He also stated that he had the following designations, Certified International Property Specialist (CIPS) and Graduate Realtor Institute (GRI). He had earned these designations; however, he did not keep up the designations' annual renewal. He also did not put the name of the brokerage on his website. The Realtor® has violated Article 12 and Standards of Practices 12.5, 12.9, and 12.13.

ARTICLE 13

> *"REALTORS® shall not engage in activities that constitute the unauthorized practice of law and shall recommend that legal counsel be obtained when the interest of any party to the transaction requires it."*

Central theme. Realtors® must not represent themselves as attorneys nor give legal advice.

Article 13 illustration. While filling out an offer to buy a piece of real property, Realtor® John was asked by his customer how they should take title to the property. John asked the question without telling his customer that they should seek legal advice. John was practicing law by answering the question and thus in violation of Article 13.

ARTICLE 14

> *"If charged with unethical practice or asked to present evidence or to cooperate in any other way, in any professional standards proceeding or investigation, REALTORS® shall place all*

pertinent facts before the proper tribunals of the Member Board or affiliated institute, society, or council in which membership is held and shall take no action to disrupt or obstruct such processes."

Central theme. Realtors® must assist the Professional Standards Committee in any investigation or hearing. They must always present the truth and not interfere with the process.

Article 14 Standards of Practice. Article 14 has four Standards of Practice:

SP 14.1 – Only one board may hear any case of alleged violations of the Code of Ethics.
SP 14.2 – A Realtor® should not disclose any information they learned at an ethics hearing.
SP 14.3 – A Realtor® should not threaten or intimidate a witness or respondent in an ethics case.
SP 14.4 – A Realtor® should not mislead the investigation into an Ethics case, nor can they file multiple charges based on the same transaction.

Article 14 illustration: Broker Alicia was named in a Code of Ethics violation. She denies the allegations. Trying to get the case canceled, Alicia threatens the person who filed the charges against her and refuses to turn over information to the Professional Standards Committee. Alicia violates Article 14 Standards of Practices 14.3 and 14.4.

==

SNAPSHOT REVIEW: UNIT FIVE

REALTORS® CODE OF ETHICS, PART II

ARTICLE 10

- Realtors® must give equal professional service to all clients and customers irrespective of race, color, religion, sex, handicap, familial status, national origin, sexual orientation, or sexual identity
- Realtors do not discriminate in their employment practices

ARTICLE 11

- Realtors® must be knowledgeable and competent in their fields of practice
- If not competent, must get assistance from a knowledgeable professional or disclose any lack of experience to their client

ARTICLE 12

- Realtors® must be honest and truthful in their communications
- must present accurate descriptions in advertising, marketing, other public representations

ARTICLE 13

- Realtors® must not engage in the unauthorized practice of law

ARTICLE 14

- Realtors® must willingly participate in an ethics investigation and enforcement actions.

Check Your Understanding Quiz:

Unit Five: Realtors® Code of Ethics, Part II

Carefully read each question then provide your best answer based on what you learned in this unit. Then check your answers against the Answer Key which immediately follows the quiz questions.

1. After attending a Professional Standards Hearing, Realtor® Adam went home and discussed the case with his wife. He told her about all the parties involved and what had happened. Then shared his opinion on what the outcome of the hearing should be. Which Article did Adam violate?

    a. Article 10
    b. Article 11
    c. Article 12
    d. Article 14

2. According to Article 13, a licensee should be careful not to practice _____,

    a. medicine
    b. law
    c. accounting
    d. appraisal

3. Realtors® may not advertise

    a. designations they have not obtained.
    b. property they have listed.
    c. a college degree.
    d. an award they won.

4. Realtors® can do appraisals. If they do an appraisal, they

    a. must follow USPAP rules and only do appraisals on Federally related transactions.
    b. need not follow USPAP rules and only appraise on a Federally related transaction.
    c. must follow USPAP rules and not appraise any Federally related transaction.
    d. need not follow USPAP rules and not appraise any Federally related transaction.

5. When is an agent able to violate Federal Fair Housing Laws?

    a. whenever it suits them
    b. never
    c. only if it is needed to make them money.
    d. only if no one suffers monetary damages.

===

Answer Key:

Unit Five: Realtors® Code of Ethics, Part II

1. d. Article 14
2. b. law
3. a. designations they have not obtained.
4. c. follow USPAP rules and not appraise any Federally related transaction.
5. b. never

Interactive Exercises

Unit 5: Realtors® Code of Ethics, Part II

SITUATIONAL CASE STUDY:

A real estate agent is involved in local politics. During the County Commission meeting, the agent made a racist comment to a black member of the Commission. After the meeting, she went to her social media accounts and made additional derogatory comments against the Commissioner. She also suggested that the county would be better off if the County Commissioner died. Based on this information, discuss this scenario and answers the questions below.

Discussion Questions:

1. Which Article of the Code of Ethics do you feel was violated in this example?
2. What specific Standard of Practice do you feel was violated?
3. How could the situation be handled without violating the Code of Ethics?

Case Debrief:

1. Article 10 of the Code of Ethics was violated.

2. The agent violated Standard of Practice 10.5.

3. The agent may state their mind in the public forum; however, she may not use slurs or hate speech. She should have remained civil and not use derogatory comments against the County Commissioner. She would be guilty because she advocated violence against the Commissioner.

UNIT 6:

REALTORS® CODE OF ETHICS, PART III

Unit Six Learning Objectives: When the student has completed this unit he or she will be able to:

- Explain the duties a Realtor® owes to other Realtors®
- Summarize the overriding thesis of the Pathway to Professionalism
- Identify the penalties for violating the Code of Ethics.
- Define and differentiate between mediation, arbitration, and the Ombudsman program.

DEFINITIONS

Arbitration

A voluntary process where an independent third party listens to the individuals involved in the dispute and makes a binding decision on who is the winner.

Mediation

A voluntary process where an independent third person helps the parties agree to resolve their dispute. Mediation is considered a win-win option; the idea is that both sides will walk out feeling they got something from the mediation. In 90 days, if no resolution is met, the parties must move on to another dispute resolution method, preferably arbitration.

Ombudsman

A voluntary process where an individual appointed by a local Board of Realtors® receives assistance to resolve disputes through constructive communication and advocating for consensus and understanding.

Procuring cause

The agent who starts the uninterrupted chain of events leading to the sale or rental of a listing.

Public trust

Public trust refers to misappropriation of client or customer funds or property, discrimination against the protected classes under the Code of Ethics, or fraud.

Duties to Realtors®

The fourth section of NAR's Code of Ethics covers how Realtors® should behave when interacting with other Realtors®. Articles 15 to 17 and their Standards of Practices identify specific behavior and guidelines for dealing with other Realtors®. This section restates many of the same ideas expressed in Articles 1 through 14; however, it explicitly identifies the duties owed to NAR members.

ARTICLE 15

" REALTORS® shall not knowingly or recklessly make false or misleading statements about other real estate professionals, their businesses, or their business practices."

Central theme. Article 15 of the Code of Ethics prohibits Realtors® from making a false or misleading statement about other real estate professionals, their own business, or their business practices.

Article 15 Standards of Practices: Article 15 three Standards of Practices as follows:

SP 15.1 – Realtors® may not file false or misleading statements about their business.

SP 15.2 – Realtors® may not make a false or misleading statement about other Realtor®. This Standard covers the false statements no matter what medium they are presented, i.e., digital, written, in person, etc.

SP 15.3 – Realtors® publish clarification if they discover a previous statement is false or misleading.

Article 15 Illustration: A Realtor® told everyone at her office that a competitive brokerage broker was not doing well financially. She even posted these statements on her Facebook page. She was trying to get agents from the other brokerage to join her company. She then boasted about how great her business was doing when in fact, it was struggling. This violation is of Article 15, Standard of Practices 15.1 and 15.2.

ARTICLE 16

" REALTORS® shall not engage in any practice or take any action inconsistent with exclusive representation or exclusive brokerage relationship agreements that other REALTORS® have with clients."

Central theme. Realtors® must not try to steal away another broker's client. If they know someone is already working with a Realtor®, they must not try and get that client to come to them.

Article 16 Standards of Practice. Article 16 has 20 Standards of Practice as follows:

SP 16.1 – This Standard of Practice serves to set boundaries a Realtor® should not cross with respect to other practitioners. It is not trying to eliminate aggressive or innovative business practices.

SP 16.2 – A Realtor® may make general statements about their business and participate in marketing campaigns without infringing on other licensees' client relationships. Standard of Practice 16.2, however, outlines two unethical types of solicitation:
1.) Telephone or personal solicitation of sellers identified by yard signs or through MLS information; and,
2.) Mail or other written solicitation sent to customers or clients of other Realtors® that are not part of a mass marketing campaign.

SP 16.3 – A Realtor® may contact a client or customer of another Realtor® to offer different services than those the client is already under contract. Realtors® cannot use MLS information to target potential customers.

SP 16.4 & 16.5 – A Realtor® should not try to steal listings or represented buyers from another agent. The only time a Realtor® may contact another Realtors® client is to get specific information not available by the other agent or not listed in the MLS.

SP16.6 – If someone under contract with another Realtor® contacts a Realtor®, the Realtor® may discuss how they would work with the customer once their contract is up with the other real estate agent.

SP16.7 – The fact that a customer has worked with a specific Realtor® in the past does not prohibit another Realtor® from trying to get hired once any existing contract has expired. People do not have to return to the same Realtor® for every transaction they complete.

SP 16.8 – The fact that an exclusive agreement existed in the past does not prohibit another Realtor® from entering into a similar agreement once the first contact expires.

SP 16.9 – Before entering into an agreement with a client, a Realtor® must ensure that the client is not already in another contract with a different Realtor®.

SP 16.10 – A buyer's agent should disclose that the agreement exists between them when they begin to negotiate a contract.

SP 16.11 – For unlisted property, Realtors® must disclose any relationship between themselves and other customers. They should also request any desired compensation at the first meeting.

SP 16.12 – All contractual relationships should be disclosed before entering into a Purchase agreement.

SP 16.13 – Realtors® should communicate to the co-broking Realtor® and not the customer or client.

SP 16.14 – A Realtor® may enter into any representation but may not require them to pay compensation if the other party is contracted to pay compensation.

SP 16.15 – All monies and compensation must be paid broker to broker.

SP 16.16 – A Realtor® may not use the terms of an offer to modify the compensation terms already laid out.

SP16.17 – Realtors® shall not attempt to extend a listing broker's offer of cooperation without the listing broker's consent.

SP 16.18 – A Realtor® shall not use information obtained from another agent or the MLS to negotiate the client away from the firm.

SP 16.19 – Realtors® must have the owner's permission before placing signs on the property.

SP 16.20 – When a Realtor® leaves a brokerage, their listing stays with the brokerage. Agents are not allowed to entice customers to follow them to another agency.

Article 16 Illustration: A Realtor® is holding an open house. A couple comes in and begins looking around. They start asking the Realtor® questions and state they want to put an offer in on the house. The agent writes up an offer and presents it to the seller, who accepts it. Only after the offer is accepted does it come out that the buyers have a Buyer's Broker Agreement with another Realtor.

The Realtor holding the open house should have asked if they were under contract with another Realtor. This is a violation of Article 16 under the Code of Ethics.

ARTICLE 17

" In the event of contractual disputes or specific non-contractual disputes as defined in Standard of Practice 17-4 between REALTORS® (principals) associated with different firms, arising out of their relationship as REALTORS®, the REALTORS® shall mediate the dispute if the Board requires its members to mediate. If the dispute is not resolved through mediation, or if mediation is not *required, REALTORS® shall submit the dispute to arbitration in accordance with the policies of the Board rather than litigate the matter.*

In the event clients of REALTORS® wish to mediate or arbitrate contractual disputes arising out of real estate transactions, REALTORS® shall mediate or arbitrate those disputes in accordance with the policies of the Board, provided the clients agree to be bound by any resulting agreement or award.

The obligation to participate in mediation and arbitration contemplated by this Article includes the obligation of REALTORS® (principals) to cause their firms to mediate and arbitrate and be bound by any resulting agreement or award."

Central theme. Realtors® should first commit to mediation if there are unsettled disputes. If mediation does not settle the conflicts, then the agents will move to binding arbitration.

Article 17 Standards of Practices: Article 17 has five Standards of Practices:

SP 17.1 – Realtors® who file litigation and refuse to withdraw in an arbitrable issue will constitute a refusal to arbitrate.

SP 17.2 – Parties to a dispute are not required to commit to mediation, but they are not relieved of the duty to arbitrate by not entering mediation.

SP 17.3 – Realtors®, when acting solely as principals, are not obligated to arbitrate disputes with other Realtors®.

SP 17.4 – This Standard of Practice lays out specific times when non-contractual disputes are subject to arbitration. Procuring cause disputes fall under this category.

SP 17.5 – The requirement to arbitrate includes disputes between Realtors® from different states. It also states which association will have jurisdiction over the disputes.

Article 17 illustration. Whenever there is a dispute among Realtors® or the parties to a real estate transaction, the parties, per our contract, should first go to mediation and then to binding arbitration. Realtors should work to keep disputes out of the legal system whenever they are able.

NAR DISPUTE RESOLUTION

Processing complaints

Anyone can file a complaint. It can be Realtor® vs. Realtor® or client/customer against Realtor®. Once filed with a local association of Realtors®, the complaint is then forwarded to the Grievance Committee to determine if there is a violation of the code of ethics and an arbitrational issue. If the Grievance Committee believes there is sufficient evidence of an Ethics violation, a hearing will be scheduled with the Professional Standards Committee to hear the case and recommend the Board of Directors on outcome and punishment.

If there is a monetary issue, then the matter will be sent to the local Board's Ombudsman program to help the parties decide. If the Ombudsman does not settle the dispute, the parties will be offered the opportunity to enter mediation and then go on to arbitration to resolve the dispute.

Penalties

Possible penalties for violation of the Code of Ethics include:

- Letter of warning;
- Letter of reprimand;
- Education courses;
- Fines not to exceed $15,000;
- Probation for not less than 30 days or more than one year;
- Membership suspension for not less than 30 days or more than one year;
- Expulsion from membership for one to three years; and/or,
- Suspension or termination of MLS rights and privileges.

PATHWAYS TO PROFESSIONALISM

While the Code of Ethics establishes enforceable standards that Realtors® must follow, it does not set out standards of common courtesy or etiquette that a Realtors® should use in their dealings with other Realtors® or the public. This is accomplished with NAR's set of professional courtesy standards called the Pathways to Professionalism.

There are three sections to the Pathways to Professionalism:

1. Respect for the Public
2. Respect for Property
3. Respect for Peers

These Professional courtesies are intended to be used by REALTORS® voluntarily. They cannot form the basis for a professional standards complaint.

Pathways to Professionalism

Respect for the Public

1. Follow the "Golden Rule": Do unto others as you would have them do unto you.
2. Respond promptly to inquiries and requests for information.
3. Schedule appointments and showings as far in advance as possible.
4. Call if you are delayed or must cancel an appointment or showing.
5. If a prospective buyer decides not to view an occupied home, promptly explain the situation to the listing broker or the occupant.
6. Communicate with all parties in a timely fashion.
7. When entering a property, ensure that unexpected situations, such as pets, are handled appropriately.
8. Leave your business card if not prohibited by local rules.
9. Never criticize property in the presence of the occupant.
10. Inform occupants that you are leaving after showings.

11. When showing an occupied home, always ring the doorbell or knock—and announce yourself loudly before entering. Knock and announce yourself loudly before entering any closed room.
12. Present a professional appearance at all times; dress appropriately and drive a clean car.
13. If occupants are home during showings, ask their permission before using the telephone or bathroom.
14. Encourage the clients of other brokers to direct questions to their agent or representative.
15. Communicate clearly; don't use jargon or slang that may not be readily understood.
16. Be aware of and respect cultural differences.
17. Show courtesy and respect to everyone.
18. Be aware of—and meet—all deadlines.
19. Promise what you can deliver—and keep your promises.
20. Identify your REALTOR® and your professional status in contacts with the public.
21. Do not tell people what you think—tell them what you know.

Respect for Property

1. Be responsible for everyone you allow to enter listed property.
2. Never allow buyers to enter listed property unaccompanied.
3. When showing property, keep all members of the group together.
4. Never allow unaccompanied access to the property without permission.
5. Enter property only with permission, even if you have a lockbox key or combination.
6. When the occupant is absent, please leave the property as you found it (lights, heating, cooling, drapes, etc.) If you think something is amiss (e.g., vandalism), contact the listing broker immediately.
7. Be considerate of the seller's property. Do not allow anyone to eat, drink, smoke, dispose of trash, use bathing or sleeping facilities, or bring pets. Leave the house as you found it unless instructed otherwise.
8. Use sidewalks; if weather is bad, take off shoes and boots inside the property.
9. Respect sellers' instructions about photographing or videographing their properties' interiors or exteriors.

Respect for Peers

1. Identify your REALTOR® and professional status in all contacts with other REALTORS®.
2. Respond to other agents' calls, faxes, and e-mails promptly and courteously.
3. Be aware that large electronic files with attachments or lengthy faxes may be a burden on recipients.
4. Notify the listing broker if there appears to be inaccurate information on the listing.
5. Share important information about a property, including pets, security systems, and whether sellers will be present during the showing.
6. Show courtesy, trust, and respect to other real estate professionals.
7. Avoid the inappropriate use of endearments or other denigrating language.
8. Do not prospect at other REALTORS®' open houses or similar events.
9. Return keys promptly.
10. Carefully replace keys in the lockbox after showings.
11. To be successful in the business, mutual respect is essential.

12. Real estate is a reputation business. What you do today may affect your reputation—and business—for years to come.

The above is from the 2021 NAR Code of Ethics and Arbitration Manual, Pathways to Professionalism, page vii. https://www.nar.realtor/code-of-ethics-and-arbitration-manual/pathways-to-professionalism

Commitment to Excellence (C2EX)

Commitment to Excellence (C2EX) from the National Association of REALTORS® empowers REALTORS® to evaluate, enhance and showcase their highest professional levels. It's not a course, class, or designation—it's an Endorsement that REALTORS® can promote when serving clients and other REALTORS®.

The NAR Board of Directors has requested that all Board of Directors, committee members, and leadership complete the C2EX program. To date, over 50,000 Realtors® have completed this program.

===

SNAPSHOT REVIEW: UNIT SIX

REALTORS® CODE OF ETHICS, PART III

SECTION FOUR OF CODE OF ETHICS

- Articles 15-17; discusses the Duties to Realtors®.

Article 15

- Realtors® must be truthful, make objective comments about other real estate professionals.

Article 16

- respect exclusive brokerage relationships of other Realtors® with their clients

Article 17

- arbitrate financial disagreements with other Realtors® and with their clients.

COMPLAINT PROCESS

- **complaint process** begins with filing of a complaint by anyone against a Realtor®.
- First, **Grievance Committee** reviews complaint, forwards to Professional Standards Committee if a violation of Code of Ethics occurred.
- **Professional Standards Committee** decides on punishment if a violation.
- recommendations forwarded to the Board of Directors to enforce

Pathway to Professionalism

- lays sets forth etiquette standards Realtors® should follow
- three categories of etiquette: Respect for the Public, Respect for Property, Respect for Peers

C2EX

- new program introduced by NAR, to date, 50,000+ Realtors® have completed program.

===

Check Your Understanding Quiz:

Unit Six: Realtors® Code of Ethics, Part III

Carefully read each question then provide your best answer based on what you learned in this unit. Then check your answers against the Answer Key which immediately follows the quiz questions.

1. Jill completed a deal with Broker Jack. She was upset with the way Jack handled the transaction. She started spreading false rumors about Jack. Jill is guilty of violating _____ of the Code of Ethics.

    a. Article 10
    b. Article 15
    c. Article 16
    d. Article 17

2. According to Article 17, a licensee should be ready to _____ any complaints filed against them.

    a. mediate
    b. ombudsman
    c. arbitrate
    d. litigate

3. Procuring cause of a sale goes to the Realtor® who

    a. listed the property.
    b. started the chain of events that lead to the sale of the property.
    c. held the open house where the buyers first saw the home.
    d. had a fiduciary duty to their client.

4. Realtors® follow the Pathway to Professionalism to show respect for

    a. the public, their peers, and their customers
    b. the public, the property, and their clients
    c. the public, the property, and their peers
    d. the property, their peers, and their customers

5. C2EX is a new program

    a. required by every Realtor®.
    b. developed by local boards.
    c. is the most recent NAR designation.
    d. allows agents to show a high level of professionalism.

===

Answer Key:

1. b. Article 15

2. c. arbitrate

3. b. started the chain of events that lead to the sale of the property.

4. c. the public, the property, and their peers

5. d. allows agents to show a high level of professionalism.

==

Interactive Exercises

Unit 6: Realtors® Code of Ethics, Part III

SITUATIONAL CASE STUDY:

Dan, who held an exclusive listing of Joey's property, invited Janet to cooperate with him. When Janet, shortly thereafter, received an offer to purchase the property and took it to Dan. Janet asked to be present at the presentation of the offer, and Dan allowed this. Together they started negotiations with the seller. The next day Janet called Joey, recommending that Joey accept the offer, which was less than the list price, and Joey agreed. The contract was signed and closed.

Discussion Questions:

1. What Article has is Janet violated?
2. What were Standards of Practices violated?
3. How could the situation be handled without violating the Code of Ethics?

Case Debrief:

1. Article 16 of the Code of Ethics was violated.
2. The agent violated Standard of Practice 16.13.
3. At the hearing, Janet defended her actions because she had been invited to present the offer to the seller and begin the negotiations to sell the property. Janet had assumed that she had Dan's permission to talk with Joey about the property's sale. The ability of a Realtor® to speak with another agent's customer must be express and not implied.

Note: Each student's opinion on how to handle this case will vary; however, each student should support their stand.

SECTION THREE:

SPECIALTY TOPICS

UNITS 7-14

Unit 7: Fair Housing, Antitrust, and Other Anti-Discrimination Laws

Unit 8: Property Management and Landlord-Tenant Relations

Unit 9: Risk Management

Unit 10: Homeowners Insurance and Flood Insurance

Unit 11: Real Estate Economics and Valuation

Unit 12: Analysis of Capital Gain and Cash Flow

Unit 13: Florida Sales Contracts

Unit 14: Pre-closing and Closing

UNIT 7:

FAIR HOUSING, ANTITRUST, AND OTHER

ANTI-DISCRIMINATION LAWS

Unit Seven Learning Objectives: When the student has completed this unit he or she will be able to:

- Define and describe the principal forms of illegal discrimination
- Identify what parties are exempt from the fair housing prohibitions
- Describe how fair housing violations are enforced
- Summarize the key provisions of the Americans with Disabilities Act
- Define and summarize the principal forms of antitrust legislation, including The Sherman Antitrust Act, Clayton Antitrust Act, collusion; price-fixing; market allocation; and tie-in agreements

PURPOSE OF FAIR HOUSING

Federal and state governments have enacted laws prohibiting discrimination in the national housing market. The aim of these fair housing laws, or equal opportunity housing laws, is to give all people in the country an equal opportunity to live wherever they wish, provided they can afford to do so, without impediments of discrimination in the purchase, sale, rental, or financing of the property.

PROTECTED CLASSES

The protected classes under Title VIII of the Civil Rights Act (known as the Fair Housing Act) as amended are:

- race
- color
- religion
- national origin
- sex
- familial status
- handicapped status

The Federal Civil Rights Act does not directly cover Sexual Orientation or Sexual Identity as protected classes; however, the U.S. Supreme Court recently ruled the LGBT community is protected under the protected class of sex.

FORMS OF PROHIBITED DISCRIMINATION

The Fair Housing Act explicitly prohibits illegal discriminatory activities in residential brokerage and financing as detailed by the following.

Discriminatory misrepresentation

An agent may not conceal available properties, represent that they are not for sale or rent, or change the sale terms in order to discriminate. For example, an agent may not inform a minority buyer that the seller has recently decided not to carry back second mortgage financing when the owner has made no such decision.

Discriminatory advertising

An agent may not advertise residential properties in such a way as to restrict their availability to any prospective buyer or tenant.

Providing unequal services

An agent may not alter the nature or quality of brokerage services to any party based on the protected classes of race, color, sex, national origin, religion, familial status, or disability. For example, if an agent typically shows a customer the latest MLS publication, the agent may not refuse to show it to any party. Similarly, if it is customary to show a qualified buyer's prospective properties immediately, an agent may not alter that practice for discriminatory purposes.

Steering

Steering is the practice of directly or indirectly channeling customers toward or away from homes and neighborhoods. Broadly interpreted, steering occurs if an agent indirectly describes an area to encourage or discourage a buyer about such an area's suitability.

For example, an agent tells Buyer A that a neighborhood is beautiful and that desirable families are moving in every week. The next day, the agent tells Buyer B that the same neighborhood is deteriorating and that home values are starting to fall. The agent has steered Buyer B away from the area and Buyer A into it.

Blockbusting

Blockbusting is the practice of inducing owners in an area to sell or rent to avoid an impending change in the ethnic or social makeup of the neighborhood that will cause values to go down.

For example, Agent Smith tells neighborhood owners that several minority families are moving into their neighborhood and that they will be bringing their relatives next year. Smith informs homeowners that several families have already made plans to move in anticipation of a value decline.

Restricting MLS participation

It is considered a discriminatory practice to limit any multiple listing service's involvements based on one's race, religion, national origin, color, sex, familial status, or disability.

Redlining

Redlining is the residential financing practice of refusing to make loans on properties in a particular neighborhood regardless of a mortgagor's qualifications. In effect, the lender draws a red line around an area on the map and denies all financing to applicants within the encircled area, usually based on the neighborhood's socioeconomic makeup.

Specific violations. Specific instances of discriminatory violations in real estate practice include:

- refusing to engage in a real estate transaction with a person
- refusing to make a transaction available
- refusing to receive or transmit an offer
- refusing to negotiate a transaction
- altering the terms, conditions, or privileges in a real estate transaction
- furnishing unequal facilities or services regarding a transaction
- falsely representing that a property is not available for inspection, sale, rental, or lease
- failing to bring a listing to a party's attention
- refusing to permit an individual to inspect a property
- indicating a preference, limitation, or discrimination based on a protected class in any advertising, record, or inquiry
- offering, soliciting, accepting, or using a real estate listing knowing that any discrimination is intended

A recent redlining case to be heard by the U.S. Supreme Court involved pizza delivery to a specific area. Domino's Pizza refused to allow its employees to deliver pizza to a particular neighborhood because their employees were being attacked and robbed. The residents of the area sued Domino's Pizza, stating that this action was a violation of the Fair Housing Law and was an example of redlining.

The Supreme Court agreed with the residents of the neighborhood that this practice was redlining. The Supreme Court told Domino's Pizza they could change policies for delivering to all areas, but they could not refuse to deliver to the specific neighborhood.

The Fairhaven Program

In 2020, NAR launched a new program on its website called Fairhaven. This program takes the agent through several different scenarios and asks them how they would handle it. It then gives feedback on the agent's responses. The program takes 60 to 90 minutes to complete. NAR recommended all agents complete the program. It is also recommended that an agent does the program multiple times, answering different ways to see how and why certain situations are illegal.

Agents must know how to answer specific questions or react to certain situations, since they can be charged and fined if they mishandle a question or problem.

Title VIII exemptions

The Fair Housing Act provides for exemptions under a few specific circumstances. These are:

- sale by the owner of a single-family home if:
  - the owner owns no more than three single-family homes, and
  - the owner or family member was the last resident, and
  - the house is sold without the use of a real estate licensee, and
  - no discriminatory ads are used
- rental of housing of four units or less if the owner resides in one of the units
- rental of rooms in a private home if owner or family member resides there or intends to live there after an absence of no more than twelve months

- local, state, or federal maximum occupancy standards
- religious organizations and not-for-profit groups in conjunction with religious organizations, if not run commercially
- rental of rooms in housing for persons of one sex
- housing for seniors

FLORIDA FAIR HOUSING LAW

Federal and state governments have both enacted laws prohibiting discrimination in the housing market. The aim of these fair housing laws, or equal opportunity housing laws, is to give all people in the country an equal opportunity to live wherever they wish, provided they can afford to do so, without impediments of discrimination in the purchase, sale, rental, or financing of real property.

In Florida, the state's Fair Housing Laws mirror the Title VIII of the 1968 Civil Rights Law, also known as Fair Housing Law. The state law can be stricter or more inclusive of the federal regulations but may not be more lenient.

Many of the counties in Florida have their own Fair Housing Laws. These can be stricter and cover broader protected groups than the State or Federal Fair Housing Laws. For example, Palm Beach County considers the LGBT community a protected class under their county's Fair Housing Guidelines; however, the State or Federal Fair Housing Acts do not explicitly include these groups of individuals.

Fair housing and local zoning

The Fair Housing Act prohibits a broad range of practices that discriminate against individuals based on race, color, religion, sex, national origin, familial status, and disability. The Act does not pre-empt local zoning laws. However, the Act applies to municipalities and other local government entities. It prohibits them from making zoning or land use decisions or implementing land-use policies that exclude or otherwise discriminate against protected persons, including individuals with disabilities.

ANTI-DISCRIMINATION ENFORCEMENT

Discrimination by the client

Fair housing laws apply to home sellers and agents, except for the exemptions previously cited. If an agent goes along with a client's discriminatory act, the agent is equally liable for violating fair housing laws. It is thus imperative to avoid complicity with client discrimination. Further, an agent should withdraw from any relationship where client discrimination occurs.

Examples of potential client discrimination are:

- refusing a full-price offer from a party
- removing the property from the market to sidestep a potential purchaser
- accepting an offer from one party that is lower than one from another party

Violations and enforcement

Persons who feel they have been discriminated against under Federal Fair Housing laws may file a complaint with the Office of Fair Housing and Equal Opportunity (FHEO) within HUD, or they may file suit in a federal or state court.

Filing an FHEO complaint

Complaints alleging fair housing violations must be filed with the Office of Fair Housing and Equal Opportunity within one year of the violation. HUD then initiates an investigation in conjunction with federal or local enforcement authorities.

If HUD decides that the complaint merits further action, it will attempt to resolve the matter out of court using conciliation. If efforts to resolve the problem fail, the aggrieved party may file suit in State or Federal court. If the case is filed in the Federal system, the Department of Justice will take over the case's prosecution.

Filing suit

In addition to or instead of filing a complaint with HUD, a party may file suit in State or Federal court within two years of the alleged violation.

Penalties

If the court finds a person guilty of discrimination, the respondent may receive various penalties, such as being enjoined or told to cease practicing. For example, a discriminating home builder may be prohibited from selling available properties to buyers. The court may also order the plaintiff to be compensated for damages, including humiliation, suffering, and pain. Also, the injured party may seek equitable relief, including forcing the guilty party to complete a denied action such as selling or renting the property. Finally, the courts may impose civil penalties for first-time or repeat offenders.

AMERICANS WITH DISABILITIES ACT

The ADA, which became law in 1990, is a civil rights law that prohibits discrimination against individuals with disabilities in all areas of public life, including employment, education, transportation, and access to facilities that are open to the general public. The purpose of the law is to make sure that people with disabilities have the same rights and opportunities.

The Americans with Disabilities Act Amendments Act (ADAAA) became effective on January 1, 2009. Among other things, the ADAAA clarified that a disability is "a physical or mental impairment that substantially limits one or more major life activities." This definition applies to all ADA titles and covers private employers with 15 or more employees, state and local governments, employment agencies, labor unions, agents of the employer, joint management-labor committees, and private entities considered places of public accommodation. Examples of the latter include hotels, restaurants, retail stores, doctor's offices, golf courses, private schools, daycare centers, health clubs, sports stadiums, and movie theaters.

ADA Titles, or Sections

The law consists of five parts, referred to as titles, as follows.

- Title I (Employment) concerns equal employment opportunity. The U.S. Equal Employment Opportunity Commission enforces Title I.
- Title II (State and Local government) concerns nondiscrimination in state and local government services. The U.S. Department of Justice enforces Title II.
- Title III (Public Accommodations) concerns nondiscrimination in public accommodations and commercial facilities. The U.S. Department of Justice enforces Title III.
- Title IV (Telecommunications) concerns accommodations in telecommunications and public service messaging. The Federal Communications Commission enforces Title IV.
- Title V (Miscellaneous) concerns various general situations, including how the ADA affects other laws, insurance providers, and lawyers.

Real estate practitioners are most likely to encounter Titles I and III, and therefore they should become familiar with these. In advising clients, licensees should make it a routine part of their practice to recommend that buyers and sellers and tenants seek qualified legal counsel.

Most people are not familiar enough with ADA Law to realize that the law only covers public, commercial, and governmental buildings; it does not directly cover residential housing. The law states that new home builders should make 5% of new construction accessible but provides no description or standards for accessibility.

Accommodating access to facilities

The ADA requires that disabled employees and members of the public be provided access to facilities that is equivalent to access afforded those who are not disabled. Specific applications include the following circumstances.

- Employers with at least fifteen employees must follow non-discriminatory employment and hiring practices.
- Reasonable accommodations must be made to enable disabled employees to perform essential functions of their jobs.
- Modifications to the physical components of the facility may be necessary to provide the required access to tenants and their customers. These include
  - widening doorways
  - changing door hardware
  - changing the way doors open
  - installing ramps
  - lowering wall-mounted telephone keypads
  - supplying Braille signage
  - providing auditory signals
- Existing barriers must be removed when the removal is "readily achievable," that is, when the cost is not prohibitive. New construction and remodeling must meet a higher standard.
- If a building or facility does not meet requirements, the landlord must determine whether restructuring or retrofitting or some other kind of accommodation is most practical.

Violations of ADA

Violations of ADA requirements can result in

- citations
- business license restrictions
- fines
- injunctions requiring remediation

Business owners may also be held liable for personal injury damages to an injured plaintiff. The Department of Justice handles federal cases involving ADA violations. They are similar to the cases previously described in this chapter for violations of Civil Rights Laws.

SNAPSHOT REVIEW: UNIT SEVEN

FAIR HOUSING, ANTI-TRUST, AND OTHER ANTI-DISCRIMINATION LAWS

PURPOSE OF FAIR HOUSING

- The purpose of the Fair Housing Act is to ensure everyone has equal housing opportunities.
- Title VIII of the 1968 Civil Rights Act = the Fair Housing Act.

PROTECTED CLASSES

- Race, Color, National Origin, Religion, Sex, Familial Status, and Handicapped Status.

FORMS OF PROHIBITED DISCRIMINATION

- Discriminatory misrepresentation
- Discriminatory advertising
- Providing unequal services
- Steering
- Blockbusting
- Restricting MLS participation
- Redlining

Title VIII exemptions

- church-owned property; private ownership of residential property; room rental; housing for seniors

FLORIDA FAIR HOUSING LAW

- mirrors Federal law; has the same protected classes.
- counties and cities permitted to have their version of Florida Fair Housing law
    - can be more inclusive than the State or Federal Law but cannot be more lenient.

ENFORCEMENT

- Complaints filed under the Federal Fair Housing Law are investigated, overseen by HUD and Department of Justice.

ADA

- ensures public areas, commercial or government buildings, transportation, education are accessible to individuals with disabilities whenever possible.
- ADA has five titles each covering a specific area.
- violations of ADA are handled same way as Fair Housing Act. Department of Justice oversees complaints and violations.

Check Your Understanding Quiz:

Chapter Seven: Fair Housing, Anti-Trust, and Other Anti-Discrimination Laws

Carefully read each question then provide your best answer based on what you learned in this unit. Then check your answers against the Answer Key which immediately follows the quiz questions.

1. Which of the following is NOT an example of discriminatory practice?

    a. Finding a home in a specifically named neighborhood
    b. Putting all customers who are black in specific neighborhoods
    c. Trying to entice homeowners to sell because a protected class is moving into the neighborhood
    d. Not providing mortgages to particular areas due to the socioeconomic makeup of the neighborhood

2. Agent Susan shows customers' homes in a particular neighborhood because she feels they would be more comfortable with people of similar race as their own. This action is an example of

    a. redlining.
    b. steering.
    c. blockbusting.
    d. normal brokerage practice.

3. Which of the following is an example of an advertisement that violates the Fair Housing Act?

    a. "Large home, perfect for a large family"
    b. "Located in a nice quiet neighborhood"
    c. "Located near shopping centers"
    d. "Many amenities nearby"

4. Which of the following is legitimately exempt from anti-discrimination laws in Florida?

    a. Housing for seniors
    b. Rental of a housing of four units or less if the owner is over 55 years of age
    c. Rental of rooms in a private home
    d. Rental of housing units with leases over one year

5. Discrimination based on race falls under

    a. Fair Housing Act, as amended in 1988
    b. Civils Rights Act of 1964
    c. Civil Rights Act of 1968
    d. Civil Rights Act of 1866

==

Answer Key:

Chapter Seven: Fair Housing, Anti-Trust, and Other Anti-Discrimination Laws

1. a. Finding a home in a specifically named neighborhood

2. b. steering

3. a. Large home, perfect for a large family

4. a. Housing for seniors

5. d. Civil Rights Act of 1866

Interactive Exercises

Chapter 7: Fair Housing, Anti-Trust, & Other Anti-Discrimination Laws

"WHAT IF" SITUATION EXAMPLE 1: Confronting Fair Housing violations/seller or buyer handling of failing contracts

As Olivia is running her morning MLS searches for clients, she notices that a new listing pops up in her neighborhood. It matches the exact criteria presented to her by her client, Jamie. Jamie falls into one of the protected classes under the Federal Fair Housing Act. Olivia doesn't want him to live in the area. She does not think he will fit in with the other neighbors, so he avoids sending him the listing.

Later on, Jamie notices the listing when he looks online and asks Olivia to see it. Olivia makes up an excuse and says there is already a pending offer. A few days go by, and the home is still marked active, so Jamie calls the listing agent, sees the house, and submits an offer without Olivia's help.

What would you do if you were Jamie?

Case Debrief:

_____

_____

_____

_____

_____

_____

_____

_____

_____

_____

Jamie should conduct some research and find out whether Olivia violated any laws. After completing the due diligence, he would discover that Olivia violated the Fair Housing Act by deliberately failing to bring a listing to his attention. He can now file a complaint with her brokerage, so she receives the appropriate disciplinary actions.

==

"WHAT IF" SITUATION EXAMPLE 2: Fair Housing questions

Mallory has been getting many calls on her current listing with questions about the home, neighborhood, etc. She was used to answering these common questions, but last Wednesday, she got a voicemail from a man named Chase who asked about the neighborhood's demographics. He wanted to know what races lived in the area and whether it was a predominantly white neighborhood. His top priority was living in a suburb that has a high white population.

He also let it be known that he is an all-cash buyer and would submit proof of funds to her as soon as he got home.

How should Mallory approach the situation? What should she say to Chase?

_____

_____

_____

_____

_____

_____

_____

_____

_____

Case Debrief:

Federal and state governments have enacted laws prohibiting discrimination in the national housing market. The aim of these fair housing laws, or equal opportunity housing laws, is to give all people in the country an equal opportunity to live wherever they wish, provided they can afford to do so, without impediments of discrimination in the purchase, sale, rental, or financing of the property. One of the protected classes under the Fair Housing Act is race. Since it is a protected class, Mallory cannot risk answering Chase's questions.

So what should she do? One way to tackle this situation is to urge Chase to complete his due diligence by running online searches on the local neighborhood's demographics. There are lots of market data available online, and Chase can discover the answers for himself without putting Mallory's license at risk.

UNIT 8:

PROPERTY MANAGEMENT AND LANDLORD-TENANT RELATIONS

Unit Eight Learning Objectives: When the student has completed this unit he or she will be able to:

- Describe the essential roles and objectives of owner and manager conducting property management business; describe the central provisions of the management agreement
- Describe the principal functions of the property manager as they relate to tenants, marketing, financial goals, and property maintenance
- Summarize the critical duties of the landlord and the tenant in an apartment rental scenario
- Describe the general process of eviction including deposit return, damages, and lease terminations

PROPERTY MANAGEMENT

Types of property manager

Property management is a specialty within the real estate profession. Real estate firms that handle the sale of commercial and investment properties are in a natural position to manage those properties for their owners. Some property managers work for firms that manage multiple properties under blanket management contracts. Others are independent agents. Some are employees of the owner. They generally fall into one of the following categories:

- **individual property manager**-- usually a real estate broker who manages properties for one for one or more owners; may belong to a small property management firm devoted to full-time property management, be self-employed, or be one of several managers in a large real estate firm.
- **individual building manager**-- usually manages a single large property; may be employed by a property manager or directly by an owner; may or may not have a real estate license.
- **resident manager (residential properties only)**-- lives on the property and may be employed by a real estate broker, a managing agent or an owner to manage a property on a part-time or full-time basis; may be required by state law for properties of certain types and sizes

A manager has a fiduciary relationship with the principal and, in general, is charged with producing the greatest possible net return on the owner's investment while safeguarding the value of the investment for the owner/investor. Professional managers are therefore much more than rent collectors. They need technical expertise in marketing, accounting, finance, and construction. Regardless of the property type managed, the manager's work involves leasing, managing, marketing, and maintaining the property.

Key management functions

Specific functions, duties, and responsibilities are determined by the management agreement, although most agreements will encompass at least the following functions.

Reporting. Financial reporting to the principal is a fundamental responsibility of the property manager. Reports may be required monthly, quarterly, and annually. Required reports typically include an annual operating budget (see below); monthly cash flow reports indicating income, expenses, net operating income, and net cash flow; profit and loss statements based on the cash flow reports and showing net profit; and budget comparison statements showing how actual results match the original budget.

Budgeting. An operating budget based on expected expenses and revenues is a necessity for management. The budget will determine rental rates, amounts available for capital expenditures, required reserve funds, salaries and wages of employees, amounts to be paid for property taxes and insurance premiums and mortgage or debt service. It will indicate the expected return, based on the previous year's performance. A typical budget will contain a projection, also based on past performance and on current market information, of income from all sources, such as rents and other services, and of expenses for all purposes, such as operating expenses, maintenance services, utilities, taxes, and capital expenditures. Operating statements itemizing income and expenses are then presented to the owner on a regular basis so that the owner can evaluate the manager's performance against the budget.

Leasing. The property manager responsibilities include seeing that the property is maintained at maximum occupancy. To achieve this, the manager may use the services of a leasing agent, whose concern is solely to rent the space. In such a situation, some of the manager's tasks may be performed by the leasing agent. Renting the property includes the following tasks, regardless of which party is actually performing them:

- **marketing**: entails advertising; brochure distribution; presentations; networking; media ads; signs; website and online services
- **setting rent levels**: entails ongoing market analysis of prevailing competitive rents in relation to amenities and building conditions
- **screening and selecting tenants**: entails credit analysis, tenant's rental history, previous landlord recommendations, employment stability, and matching tenant needs with features of the property.
- **collecting rents:** entails enforcing the terms of the lease, particularly the tenant's financial obligations. Here the manager must comply with legal procedures for collecting delinquent rents. The manager must also understand how to properly handle deposits and advance rent payments.
- **maintain harmonious tenant relations**: entails regular communications with tenants; responding promptly and satisfactorily to maintenance and service requests; enforcing rules and lease terms consistently and fairly; and complying with all relevant laws, such as fair housing and ADA (Americans with Disabilities Act) regulations

Property maintenance. Physical maintenance of the property is one of the property manager's primary functions. The costs of services provided must always be balanced with financial objectives and the need to satisfy tenant needs. The manager will also be concerned with staffing and scheduling requirements, in accordance with maintenance objectives.

Routine maintenance activities are those necessary for the day-to-day functioning of the property. Regular performance of these activities helps to keep tenants satisfied as well as forestall serious problems requiring repair or correction. Routine activities are such things as:

- regular inspections
- scheduled upkeep of mechanical systems-heating, air-conditioning, rest rooms, lighting, landscaping
- regular cleaning of common areas
- minor repairs
- supervision of purchasing

Construction projects

On a less-regular basis the property manager must take on various construction projects needed to maintain the property in operating, competitive condition. These projects generally fall into three categories: tenant improvements, renovations, and environmental issues.

Tenant improvements. Alterations made specifically for certain tenants are called build-outs or tenant improvements. The work may involve merely painting and re-carpeting a rental space, or erecting new walls and installing special electrical or other systems. In new buildings, spaces are often left incomplete so that they can be finished to an individual tenant's specifications. In such cases, it is important to clarify which improvements will be considered tenant property (trade fixtures) and which will belong to the building.

Renovations. When buildings lose functionality, or become functionally obsolescent, they generally also lose tenants, drop in class, and suffer declining rental rates. Renovation may solve some of these problems, but the manager will have to help the owner determine whether the costs of renovation can be recovered by increased revenues resulting from the improvements.

Environmental remediations. A variety of environmental concerns confronts a property manager, ranging from air quality to waste disposal, tenant concerns, and federal, state and local environmental regulations. The managed property may contain asbestos, radon, mold, lead, and other problematic substances. Tenants may produce hazardous waste. The manager must be aware of the issues and see that proper procedures are in place to deal with them, including providing means for proper disposal of hazardous materials, arranging for environmental audits and undertaking possible remediation.

The management agreement

The management agreement establishes an agency agreement between manager and owner as well as specifying such essentials as the manager's scope of authority, responsibilities, objectives, compensation, and the term of the agreement. Property managers are usually considered to be general agents empowered to perform some or all of the ongoing tasks and duties of operating the property, including the authority to enter into contracts.

The contractual relationship effected by the management agreement ensures that the manager will strive to realize the highest return for the owner consistent with the owner's objectives and instructions. The agreement should be in writing and include at least the basics of any real estate contract, as follows

- **Names of the parties**--owner, landlord, manager, tenant or other party to be bound by the contract
- **Property description**--street address, unit number and location, square footage, and other information that specifies the leased premises
- **Term**--time period (**months**, years) covered by the contract; termination conditions and provisions
- **Owner's purpose**--**maximize** net income, maximize asset value, maximize return, minimize expenditure, maintain property quality, etc.; long-term goals for the property
- **Owner's responsibilities**--**management** fees, plus any management expenses such as payroll, advertising and insurance that the manager will not be expected to pay
- **Manager's authority**--the **scope** of powers being conveyed to the manager: hiring and staffing, setting rents, contracting with vendors, ordering repairs, limits on expenditures without seeking owner permission
- **Manager's responsibilities**--**specification** of duties, such as marketing, leasing, maintenance, budgeting, reporting, collecting and handling rents; the manager should be included as an additional insured on the liability policy for the property
- **Budget**--amounts, or percentages of revenues, allotted for operations, taxes, insurance, capital expenditures, etc.
- **Reporting**--how often and what kind of reports are to be made
- **Compensation**--the management fee or other means of compensation to the manager

Licensing requirements

Property managers managing property for others for a commission must have an active brokers license in order to practice, as renting and leasing are considered licensed activities. In addition, a Florida property management company must also have a license.

On the other hand, individuals or business entities may manage their own properties without the requirement to obtain a license.

Note further that if the property owner hires a salaried manager as an employee, such a manager does not have to be licensed.

FLORIDA FAIR HOUSING ACT

Protected classes

Florida Statute Title XLIV, Chapter 760, Section 20, known as the Florida Fair Housing Act, protects seven classes: race, color, religion, sex, national origin, disability, and familial status. Marital status, age, and occupation are not covered.

Discrimination illustrated

The following acts illustrate discrimination and are prohibited by the Florida Fair Housing Act:

- A prospective tenant is told on the telephone that an apartment rents for a certain price and is currently available but then, when meeting the landlord face to face, is told the rental price is higher or the apartment is no longer available when it is still available.

- A condominium association refuses to provide handicapped parking for a person with a disability.
- A landlord enforces a no pets policy when the prospective tenant has a service dog.
- A homeowner refuses to sell property to a member of any of the protected classes.
- A real estate licensee encourages a buyer to purchase a particular house because it is located in a specific religious community.
- A landlord refuses to rent to a single woman who is pregnant.

In each case there is discrimination characterized by preferential treatment, denial of services, or illegal denial of real property.

Complaints

In Florida, discrimination victims may file a complaint with the Florida Commission on Human Relations and/or HUD within 1 year of the alleged discrimination. Further, he or she may file a civil lawsuit within 2 years of the alleged discrimination. If the court finds in favor of the complainant, a fine up to $10,000 may be imposed on a first-time violator or up to $25,000 on a repeat violator within the previous 5 years.

FLORIDA RESIDENTIAL LANDLORD AND TENANT ACT

The Florida Residential Landlord and Tenant Act (FRLTA) applies to the rental of a residential dwelling and provides regulations for all aspects of residential rental occupancies. It does not apply to rent-to-own contracts where required funds have been paid. Nor does it apply to transient occupancy in public lodging or occupancy in a cooperative unit or condominium unit. Under the Act, provisions within a rental agreement that violate the FRLTA are not enforceable.

Landlord obligations

Deposits and advance rents. Landlords may require a security deposit and advanced rent payments (typically the last month's rent). In Florida, there is no limit on the amount of deposit landlords can charge, but they must comply with the Act in how they handle deposits and advanced rent payments.

Either in the lease agreement or within 30 days of receiving the security deposit and advance rent, the landlord is required to give the tenant written notice of the advance rent or security deposit.

Landlord's obligation to maintain premises. Landlords are required to comply with building, housing, and health codes in maintaining the rental property. If none of these codes exist, the landlord is required to keep the premises in good repair and maintain systems such as plumbing and heating in working condition.

The Act specifically states that window screens must be installed and kept in good repair, pests must be exterminated, and garbage is to be removed with outside receptacles provided. The landlord must also install smoke detectors in single family or duplex rental homes.

The landlord may charge the tenant for garbage removal, water, fuel, or utilities if included in the lease. The landlord is not responsible for conditions caused by negligence or wrongful acts of the tenant, family members, or guests.

Landlord's access to premises. The landlord is permitted by law to enter the rental unit from time to time for inspections, repairs, alterations, supplying services, or show the unit to prospective tenants or buyers. The landlord is required to give the tenant at least 12 hours' notice prior to entry for repairs and may only enter between 7:30 a.m. and 8:00 p.m.

Tenant obligations

The tenant is obligated to comply with applicable building, housing, and health codes. The tenant must also keep the premises clean and sanitary, including removing garbage, cleaning plumbing fixtures, and operating the dwelling's systems in a reasonable manner. Similarly, tenants are obligated to conduct themselves so as not to disturb neighbors and refrain from damaging or removing any part of the premises that belongs to the landlord.

Tenancy termination

Tenant termination. The tenant may terminate the rental agreement if the landlord fails to maintain the premises as required by law or fails to comply with the provisions in the rental agreement. To do so, the tenant needs to deliver a written 7-day notice to the landlord specifying the noncompliance and stating the intention to terminate. If the landlord does not correct the noncompliance within the 7 days, the tenant may terminate the rental agreement.

Landlord termination. The landlord may terminate the rental agreement if the tenant fails to comply with tenant obligations or fails to comply with the provisions of the agreement. The landlord must deliver a written 7-day notice to the tenant specifying the noncompliance and stating the intention to terminate. If the tenant does not correct the noncompliance within the 7 days, the landlord may terminate the rental agreement.

- **Non-payment of rent.** If the tenant's noncompliance is nonpayment of rent, the landlord must give the tenant written notice of the requirement to pay the rent or vacate the premises within 3 business days. If the tenant still does not pay the rent after the 3 days, the landlord may terminate the rental agreement.

Eviction

A landlord who needs to remove a tenant from the rental unit must follow the procedure mandated by Florida statute, as follows.

- After serving the tenant notice to vacate the premises, the landlord must give the tenant 3 business days to vacate for not paying rent or 7 days to vacate for other noncompliance issues.
- If the tenant does not vacate in the allowed timeframe, the landlord, the landlord's attorney, or the landlord's agent must file a complaint in the local county court that describes the rental unit and the reason it needs to be recovered. A copy of the complaint is delivered to the tenant by the local sheriff's department.
- If the tenant files a response to the complaint, the court's clerk will notify the tenant that he or she has 5 business days to pay the rent into the court's registry.

- If the tenant fails to respond to the court's notice within the 5 business days, the landlord is entitled to an immediate default judgment for removal of the tenant without further notice or hearing.
- After the judgment has been issued in favor of the landlord, the clerk will issue a writ to the sheriff instructing the sheriff to post a 24-hour notice on the premises and then give possession of the unit to the landlord.
- After the sheriff signs the writ of possession, the landlord or the landlord's agent may remove the tenant's personal property remaining on the premises. The landlord may have the sheriff stand by to keep the peace while locks are changed and personal items are removed. The tenant may not hold the sheriff, the landlord, or the landlord's agent liable for any loss or damage to the property after it is removed.

If the eviction is a result of nonpayment of rent and the court finds in favor of the landlord, the court will enter a money judgment against the tenant that includes the amount of rent due and may include attorney's fees and costs. Until all money due is paid, the landlord will hold a lien against the all of the tenant's property, except beds, bedclothes, and wearing apparel (F.S. 83.09).

===

SNAPSHOT REVIEW: UNIT EIGHT

PROPERTY MANAGEMENT AND LANDLORD-TENANT RELATIONS

PROPERTY MANAGEMENT

Types of property manager
- Individual property manager -- real estate broker who manages properties for 1+ owners
- Individual building manager -- manages a single large property
- Resident manager – resides on site; may be employed by real estate broker, managing agent or owner to manage property part-time or full-time

Key management functions
- Financial reporting to principal
- Managing operating budget based on expected expenses and revenues
- Maintain tenancy levels at maximum occupancy
- Maintain physical aspects of property; repairs

Construction projects
- Tenant improvements-alterations made specifically for certain tenants; painting, re-carpeting, installing special electrical systems
- Property manager determines whether costs of renovation can be recovered by increased revenues resulting from improvements
- Property manager must be aware of environmental issues and see that procedures are in place to deal with them

The management agreement
- Establishes agency agreement between manager and owner
- Specifies manager's scope of authority, responsibilities, objectives, compensation, and term of agreement

Licensing requirements
- Property managers managing property for others for commission must have active brokers license

FLORIDA FAIR HOUSING ACT

Protected classes
- Race, color, religion, sec, national origin, disability, and familial status
- Marital status, age, occupation not protected

Discrimination variations
- Preferential treatment, denial of services; illegal denial of real property

Complaints
- Discrimination victims may file complaint with Florida Commission on Human Relations and/or HUD; must be within 1 year of alleged discrimination violation

FLORIDA RESIDENTIAL LANDLORD AND TENANT ACT

- Applies to rental of residential dwellings and provides regulations for all aspects of residential rental occupancies

Landlord obligations

- May require security deposit and advanced rent payments
- Comply with building, housing, health codes
- Permitted by law to enter the rental unit from time to time for inspections, repairs, alterations, supplying services, or show unit to prospective tenants or buyers
- Must give tenant at least 12 hours' notice prior to entry

Tenant obligations

- Comply with applicable building, housing, and health codes; maintain cleanliness of premises

Tenancy termination

- Tenant may terminate rental agreement if landlord fails to maintain premises as required by law or fails to comply with provisions in rental agreement

Eviction

- Landlord must follow procedure mandated by Florida statute to remove tenant from rental unit

Check Your Understanding Quiz:

Unit Eight: Property Management and Landlord-Tenant Relations

Carefully read each question then provide your best answer based on what you learned in this unit. Then check your answers against the Answer Key which immediately follows the quiz questions.

1. Which type of property manager typically lives on the property he or she manages?

   a. Resident manager
   b. Individual manager
   c. Building manager
   d. Commercial property manager

2. Which of the following statements is true?

   a. Property management companies are exempt from licensure..
   b. Florida property management companies must have a license.
   c. A salaried property manager has to be licensed.
   d. A property manager can only be paid by commission.

3. Which of the following is a landlord's obligation?

   a. The landlord needs to remove garbage from the property.
   b. The landlord must clean plumbing fixtures.
   c. The landlord needs to keep the premises clean.
   d. The landlord must maintain the plumbing in working condition.

4. Which of the following steps comes first in the eviction process?

   a. The landlord must give the tenant 3 business days to vacate.
   b. The landlord must file a complaint in the local county court.
   c. The landlord must serve the tenant notice to vacate the premises.
   d. The clerk must issue a writ to instruct the sheriff to post a 24-hour notice on the premises.

5. Which of the following is a responsibility of the property manager?

   a. Marketing the property
   b. Payroll
   c. Advertising costs
   d. Property insurance costs

6. Which of the following is a protected class under the Florida Fair Housing Act?

   a. Occupation
   b. Lack of education
   c. Low income level
   d. Disability

===

Answer Key:

Unit Eight: Property Management and Landlord-Tenant Relations

1. a. Resident manager

2. b. Florida property management companies must have a license

3. d. The landlord must maintain the plumbing in working condition.

4. c. The landlord must serve the tenant notice to vacate the premises.

5. a. Marketing the property

6. d. Disability

UNIT 9:

RISK MANAGEMENT

Unit Nine Learning Objectives: When the student has completed this unit he or she will be able to:

- Identify numerous ways to capitalize on risk reduction via the adoption of key risk management strategies
- Summarize significant areas of risk encountered by licensees in the ordinary discharge of their brokerage activities

RISK MANAGEMENT STRATEGIES

Risk is the chance of losing something. Its two dimensions are the probability of occurrence and the extent of exposure to monetary or non-monetary consequences. Since most risks are related to judgments and decisions, the real estate licensee, who makes numerous complex decisions every day, faces a high degree of risk potential.

Risk management is a structured approach to dealing with the uncertainties and consequences of risk. In real estate practice, the aim is to reduce risk to an acceptable level through anticipation and planning.

Well-established strategies for managing risk are:

- Avoidance (elimination)
- Reduction (mitigation, sharing)
- Transference (outsourcing, insuring)

Avoidance

Avoidance includes refraining from an activity that carries risk. Complete avoidance of risk in real estate practice is almost impossible. A broker, for instance, may believe that hiring only experienced affiliates eliminates the risk that affiliates will commit license law violations. However, even experienced practitioners may not know the law, and, sometimes, people break the law deliberately. The risk may be reduced, but it remains. Perhaps a better example is bragging about a neighborhood and how the homes in it are virtually assured to enjoy a very high degree of appreciation. That form of exaggeration creates an unnecessary risk that the licensee will be sued when such appreciation doesn't happen. The lesson is to avoid indefensible claims using the avoidance strategy.

Reduction

Employing the reduction strategy involves taking steps to reduce the probability or the severity of a potential loss. A familiar example is a sprinkler system that dispenses water to reduce the risk of fire.

In real estate practice, one risk reduction tactic is to share responsibility for making a decision. The agent provides the consumer with expertise, and perhaps some advice, but lets the consumer decide how much to offer. In this way, the agent gets some relief from the risks inherent in the buyer's decision to purchase.

Transference

Transference means passing the risk to another party, by contract or other means. An insurance policy is the common example. In the real estate business, transference is typically and most successfully accomplished by means of an errors and omissions (E&O) insurance policy, either on the individuals in a firm or on the firm itself. Another form of transference is recommending licensed specialists to provide advice rather than offering one's own opinion. This strategy commonly comes into play when disclosing the condition of a property. Beyond the superficialities of what the eye can see, there are numerous issues that a professional inspector might unveil. Using licensed inspectors transfers the risk of a licensee's liability in representing property condition to the professional inspector.

RISK MANAGEMENT TACTICAL PROCEDURES

Experience shows that the most common strategies for risk management in real estate practice are reduction and transference. To effect these strategies, the licensee can adopt effective, practical tactics or actions in actual practice. These include:

- education
- disclosure
- documentation
- insurance

Education

Education is the first line of defense against risk. When agents are familiar with the forms provided by the office, how and when to complete them and where to send them, the likelihood of errors is reduced. Likewise, agents need to be able to identify and understand common contract elements, complete contract forms developed by attorneys, and refrain from offering legal opinions.

In Florida, brokers have a legal obligation to provide supervision of affiliated licensees, which also implies compliance training. In addition, licensees must satisfy legal requirements for continuing education, while those who care about personal excellence will seek further education and training to enhance their professional skills.

Disclosure

Licensees have the duty to ensure that all parties have the information they are entitled to via required disclosures. Proper disclosure in turn reduces the risk that clients and customers will accuse a licensee of misleading or inducing them to make a decision with incomplete information.

Disclosure may be made in writing or verbally and may or may not require written acknowledgment from the receiving party. Required disclosures include those that clarify:

- agency relationships
- property condition

- duties and obligations of licensees
- whether a licensee has a personal interest in a transaction
- material facts that affect the decision-making of the client

Documentation

Documentation provides evidence of compliance with laws and regulations. It proves what clients and customers and licensees said and did in a transaction. Some documentation is required by law.

The components of a thoroughly documented paper trail include:

- standard Realtor® or broker-approved forms
- communication records
- transaction records
- contracts
- trust records
- promulgated transaction addenda

Policy and procedures manual. A written and uniformly enforced company policy manual lets everyone in the firm know what to expect before problems arise. The policy manual should cover the company's rules in such areas as floor duty privileges, assignment of relocation properties to agents, referrals between agents within the company, and requirements for continuing education, sales meeting participation, and property tours.

Company procedures in the P&P manual should spell out how to handle every aspect of the company's business that agents and brokers need to know—from handling consumers' funds and documents, conducting consumer transactions, dealing with MLS-related matters, and placing signage, to all procedures prescribed by state or federal law, especially license, banking and fair housing laws. Whenever changes are made to the P&P manual, each agent should sign the revised manual as evidence that the agent has examined it.

Standard forms. Standard forms save time and protect against the unauthorized practice of law. Since they are most often prepared by lawyers familiar with the market area, they can address contingencies that are common in the area in a manner that reflects the real estate laws of the state. On the other hand, a licensee often needs to adapt a standardized form for a client by assisting with filling in blanks, modifying terms, and attaching addenda. The licensee must always remain aware of the limitations the state has placed on performing such activities without a law license.

Transaction records. State laws require licensees to document transactions. Firms are required to keep written records of all real estate transactions for a specific time period after closing or termination. Document retention is inherently a primary risk management tactic in addition to being mandated by FREC.

Insurance

Many forms of insurance are available for property owners and managers. Some of these types are also used to manage certain risks of brokers and licensees.

General Liability. General liability insurance provides coverage for risks incurred by a property owner when the public or a licensee enters the owned property (public liability). The insurer pays the covered claim and legal fees, costs, and expenses, including medical expenses, resulting from owner negligence or other causes. This type of insurance does not cover professional liability, for which an Errors & Omissions policy is necessary.

Errors and Omissions. Professional liability is of two general types:

- Unprofessional conduct – a claim that one has failed to carry out fiduciary duties and provide an acceptable standard of care
- Breach of contract – a claim that one has failed to perform services under the terms of a contract in a timely manner

The primary method for transferring the professional liability risks of brokers, managers, and licensees is Errors & Omissions (E&O) insurance. A standard E&O policy provides coverage for "damages resulting from any negligent act, error or omission arising out of Professional Services."

A standard policy does NOT cover:

- violations of law
- fraudulent, dishonest, criminal or malicious acts
- mishandling of escrow moneys, earnest money deposits, or security deposits
- antitrust violations
- sexual harassment
- Fair Housing violations
- agent-owned properties
- environmental violations
- failure to detect or disclose environmental conditions, including mold
- acts committed prior to licensure or after termination of active status
- activities as an appraiser if licensing other than a real estate license is required

E&O insurance, in short, covers "mistakes" but not crimes. It is an outstanding risk management tactic – but it has very tangible limitations.

RISK MANAGEMENT IN PRACTICE

Agency

The risks involved in agency relationships generally will occur in one of two areas:

- the requirement to inform and disclose
- the requirement to carry out an agency duty.

In Florida agency relationships are in writing and must be disclosed to all parties to a transaction. State law may spell out agency duties, or the duties may be a part of general agency law. In states that do not use agency, there is still the obligation to explain and disclose the nature of the relationship.

Disclosure requirements. A licensee may be acting in a transaction as facilitator, agent, subagent, designated agent, single agent, dual agent, non-agent or in some capacity. Regardless of status, the licensee must follow state disclosure requirements. These are, typically, to:

- disclose status verbally to other licensees on initial contact
- disclose status verbally to buyer and seller before providing real estate services
- confirm the disclosure in writing before signing a listing agreement or presenting a purchase offer (to an unrepresented seller) or before preparing a purchase offer (to an unrepresented buyer)
- get a signed receipt indicating the written disclosure has been made

Carrying out the duties of agency also require disclosures of :

- personal interest the agent has in a transaction (such as owner or buyer)
- personal benefit the agent will derive from a service referral
- required property and market information
- information about customers a client is entitled to have

The key to good risk management practice in brokerage relationships is to "put everything on the table" at the earliest opportunity. This applies to disclosing the nature of the relationship to the prospective client and to subsequent customers.

Conflicts of interest

Conflicts of interest arise when an agent forgets to put the best interests of a client ahead of those of everyone else. This can happen in situations involving undisclosed dual agencies, broker-owned listings, licensees buying for their own account, vendor referrals, and property management subcontracting of services, among many others. Even ordinary, everyday transactions carry a built-in risk of conflict of interest. Consider the fact that a licensee usually receives no compensation for a failed transaction. Therefore, it is in the licensee's interest to see the transaction completed, even if it may not be in the client's best interest. A negative result from a home inspection or other test has the potential to cause a buyer to back out of a contract. A licensee who has forgotten whose best interest should be primary might be tempted to recommend inspectors who will overlook problems in exchange for receiving

referrals. Licensees must always disclose any self-interest they have in a transaction, and always remember their duties to clients and consumers.

Property disclosures

Property condition. Florida requires the seller of a residential property to deliver to the buyer a written disclosure or disclaimer about the property's condition, including any material defects the owner knows about. The disclosure is required before any purchase contract is accepted. The licensee should always obtain the parties' signatures acknowledging receipt of these disclosures.

Generally the licensee has no further duty to disclose property condition after properly informing parties of their rights and obligations. However, the licensee may still be subject to legal action for

- deliberately distorting the facts (intentional misrepresentation)
- cheating any party (fraud)

- concealing or failing to disclose adverse facts which the licensee knew about or should have known about (intentional or unintentional misrepresentation)

Comparative Market Analysis (CMA).

In preparing a Comparative Market Analysis, licensees should guard against using the terms "appraisal" and "value," which are reserved for the use of certified appraisers. Misuse of these terms could lead to a charge of misrepresenting oneself as an appraiser. In discussing listed properties with clients or customers, real estate licensees should be careful to use guarded terms such as "recommended listing price," "recommended purchase price,' and "recommended listing price range."

Agents should make every effort to help the sellers find a reasonable listing price based on the current market. If the CMA leads the seller to list at a price that is too high, the seller may blame the agent when the transaction fails because of an appraisal that comes in below the selling price. To minimize this risk, it is best to be conservative in the CMA and retain documentation that the seller went above the recommended price in spite of the agent's advice.

Estimate of Closing Costs

In preparing an estimate of closing costs for a seller or buyer, there is the risk of forgetting something, leading to an unpleasant surprise when the consumer suddenly faces unexpected costs or conditions. Licensees should use their broker's form, if there is one, and make it clear to the consumer that it is only an estimate of likely costs, not a statement of actual costs. In some states, brokers and agents do not prepare closing cost estimates, leaving that task to the lender.

Advertising

State and federal laws regulate advertising, including the federal Fair Housing laws as they pertain to discriminatory advertising and providing of services. Advertising includes electronic communication, social media/networking, and internet marketing. Usage must be consistent with company image and legal requirements. The license laws of most states list illegal advertising actions subject to discipline such as:

- making any substantial and intentional misrepresentation
- making any promise that might cause a person to enter into a contract or agreement when the promise is one the licensee cannot or will not abide by
- making continued and blatant misrepresentations or false promises through affiliate brokers, other persons, or any advertising medium
- making misleading or untruthful statements in any advertising, including using the term "Realtor" when not authorized to do so and using any other trade name, insignia or membership in a real estate organization when the licensee is not a member.

Authorizations and Permissions. Licensees should stay within the bounds of the authority granted by the agency agreement or must not do anything requiring permission without first getting that permission in writing. For instance, permission should be obtained before doing any of the following unless the listing agreement specifically grants the authority:

- post a sign on the property

- remove other signs
- show the property
- hand out the property condition disclosure
- distribute marketing materials
- use a multiple listing service
- cooperate with other licensees
- divide the commission or negotiate a commission split
- share final sales data with the MLS
- place a lock box on the property

Scope of expertise

Real estate licensees are not, by nature, financial consultants, accountants, appraisers, soil scientists, well-diggers, lawyers, decorators, contractors, builders, plumbers, carpenters, inspectors, , and a number of other kinds of expert. However, in today's competitive environment, consumers often demand much more from a licensee than the traditional basic services. An agent who fails to live up to prevailing standards may be held liable for negligence, fraud, or violation of state real estate license laws and regulations. At the same time, agents must be particularly careful about the temptation to misrepresent themselves as experts and offer inappropriate expert advice.

Disclaiming one's expertise and referring parties to specialized professionals are always the best risk control procedures. This practice avoids being accused of misrepresentation from a consumer who claims to have been harmed by reliance on the licensee's non-existent expertise. The exact nature of the licensee's services to be provided should be stated as clearly as possible in the listing agreement.

Contracting process

According to the Statute of Frauds, all contacts for real estate must be in writing to be enforceable. Contracts that contain incorrect information or are inadequately prepared can pose a serious liability for a licensee. To avoid such a situation, it is imperative for the contract to reflect the terms that the parties have agreed upon in the most accurate and honest manner.

Common risks and errors in the contracting process include:

- using an illegal form

  A licensee may be punished for using any real estate listing agreement form, sales contract form, or offer to purchase form that lacks a definite termination date.

- failing to state inclusions and exclusions

  The parties should identify as included in or excluded from the transfer any ambiguous items. Unwritten agreements between the parties are a source of later dispute and trouble.

- failing to track the progress of contingency satisfaction

  The time period for completing contingencies such as inspections is specific and limited. Failure to meet or waive a condition may terminate the contract. A "time is of the essence" clause in the standard agreement makes the time period for contingencies critical.

- mistakes in entering data in a form

All data should be checked and verified: dates, times, amounts, warranties, descriptions, names, representations, promises, procedures, authority, etc. One way to reduce risk in the contracting process is to use a checklist that covers all the contract items.

Rules and regulations

Florida real estate laws and regulations attempt to cover every principal threat to the public safety when involved in real estate brokerage. Violations of these strictures represents a direct threat to the legal and financial status of licensee. The following prohibitions should be carefully observed in implementing one's risk management strategies:

- obtaining a license under false pretenses
- committing a "prohibited act"
- neglecting to present every written offer as required
- neglecting to deliver signed copies of accepted offers to transaction parties as required
- failing to make sure that all required terms and conditions are present in a contract to purchase
- handling earnest money and other escrow funds improperly
- acting without a license when a license is required
- demanding a referral fee without reasonable cause
- entering into a net listing
- trying to induce another licensee's client to end or change an existing agency contract
- paying a commission to an unlicensed individual or company
- receiving an illegal referral fee, rebate or kickback
- practicing with an expired license

Referring service providers

There are several risks attending the recommendation of vendors and service providers to a consumer. First, the consumer may not be satisfied with the performance of the recommended party and blame the licensee. Second, in cases where a recommended provider performs illegal acts, there may be legal consequences for the licensee. Third, if a licensee has a business relationship with a recommended vendor or provider and neglects to disclose the fact, there are legal consequences.

The major risk management technique in referring service providers is to shift the responsibility for choosing a vendor to the consumer. This can be done

- by refusing to recommend vendors at all
- by presenting a broad range of choices and allowing the consumer to select; or
- by presenting a short list of thoroughly vetted vendors and allowing the consumer to make the decision

In addition, licensees should include the disclaimer that, to the best of the licensee's knowledge, the vendors on the list are competent and honest, but that the consumer is responsible for investigating and making his or her own judgment before hiring or buying.

SNAPSHOT REVIEW: UNIT NINE

RISK MANAGEMENT

RISK MANAGEMENT STRATEGIES

- Overriding purpose is to mitigate uncertainties and consequences of risk incurred in the normal course of real estate practice

Avoidance
- Refraining from activity that carries risk

Reduction
- Taking steps to reduce probability or severity of potential loss

Transference
- Passing risk to another party by contract or other means
- Errors and Omissions insurance helps accomplish transference

RISK MANAGEMENT TACTICAL PROCEDURES

- Most common strategies for risk management are reduction and transference

Education
- Familiarity with forms provided by the office, how and when to complete and where to send them, likelihood of errors is reduced

Disclosure
- Licensees have duty to ensure all parties have information they're entitled to via required disclosures
- Proper disclosure reduces risk clients and customers will accuse a licensee of misleading or inducing them to make decisions with incomplete information

Documentation
- Provides evidence of compliance with laws and regulations
- Policy and procedures manual generally mandates license law regulations as company policy
- Standardized forms save time and protect against unauthorized practice of law
- Address contingencies that are common in area
- Transaction records -- required by state law to document transactions
- Firms required to keep written records of real estate transactions for specific time period after closing or termination

Insurance
- Some used to manage certain risks of brokers and licensees
- General liability insurance covers risks incurred by property owner when public or licensee enters the owned property

Errors and Omissions
- Coverage for "damages resulting from any negligent act, error or omission arising out of Professional Services"

RISK MANAGEMENT IN PRACTICE

Agency
- Risks in agency relationships generally in requirement to inform, disclose or carry out agency duty

Conflicts of interest
- When agent forgets to put best interests of client ahead of everyone else

Property disclosures
- Seller must deliver written disclosure or disclaimer about property's condition, including material defects owner knows about

Comparative Market Analysis
- Guard against terms "appraisal" and "value" in preparation of CMA

Estimate of closing costs
- Use broker's form and make it clear to consumer that it is estimate

Advertising
- Electronic communication, social media/networking, internet marketing
- Must be consistent with company image and legal requirements

Authorizations and permissions
- Licensees should stay within bounds of authority granted by agency agreement

Scope of expertise
- Agents must be careful about temptation to misrepresent themselves as experts

Contracting process
- Contracts must be in writing to be enforceable
- Must reflect terms that parties agreed upon in most accurate and honest manner

Rules and regulations
- Florida real estate laws and regulations attempt to cover every principal threat to public safety when involved in real estate brokerage

Referring service providers
- Shift responsibility of choosing a vendor to consumer
- Licensees can refuse to recommend vendors, present broad range of choices and allow consumer to select, or present short list of vetted vendors
- Include disclaimer-consumer
- Responsible for making own judgment before hiring or buying

===

Check Your Understanding Quiz:

Unit Nine: Risk Management

Carefully read each question then provide your best answer based on what you learned in this unit. Then check your answers against the Answer Key which immediately follows the quiz questions.

1. Well-established strategies for managing risk are: avoidance, reduction and _____.

    a. illumination.
    b. discrimination.
    c. meticulousness.
    d. transference.

2. Which of the following is a form of professional liability?

    a. Standardized contracts
    b. Recommending customers use an attorney
    c. Completing an offer for a client
    d. Professional conduct

3. What word(s) should licensees avoid using when preparing a CMA?

    a. Appraisal
    b. Market analysis
    c. Comparative analysis
    d. Comparable

4. Which risk strategy involves taking steps to reduce the probability of a potential loss?

    a. Retention
    b. Projecting appreciation
    c. Avoidance
    d. Procuring cause

5. Which statute requires all real estate contracts to be in writing to be enforceable?

    a. Written Statute
    b. Law of Contracts
    c. Statute of Frauds
    d. Statute of Articulation

6. Which of the following does a standard E&O policy cover?

    a. Damages resulting from any negligent act
    b. Violations of law
    c. Antitrust violations
    d. Fraudulent acts

==

Answer Key:

Unit Nine: Risk Management

1. d.   transference.

2. c.   Completing contract

3. a.   Appraisal

4. b.   Reduction

5. c.   Statute of Frauds

6. a.   Damages resulting from any negligent act

UNIT 10:

HOMEOWNERS INSURANCE AND FLOOD INSURANCE

Unit Ten Learning Objectives: When the student has completed this unit he or she will be able to:

- Describe the purpose and types of homeowners insurance policies and the related range of coverages offered by such policies
- Generally characterize the distinctions between HO-I through HO-8 homeowners' policies
- Describe the nature and purpose of flood insurance and how it is impacted by flood zones and federal FEMA regulations
- Characterize the licensee's disclosure obligations with respect to flood insurance

PURPOSE

The purpose of insurance is to protect an asset against possible loss, whether that loss be related to property, flood, auto, health, business, life or pets. Some types of insurance are required because of where one lives and what one owns. For example, most mortgage lenders require homeowner's insurance to protect a property that is collateral for the lender's loan. A lender may require flood insurance on a property located in a flood zone.

In the world of real estate, the types of insurance of most common concern are homeowners' insurance and flood insurance.

HOMEOWNERS INSURANCE ESSENTIALS

Lender-placed v owner-placed insurance

Lender-placed insurance. Most lenders will place homeowner's insurance on a home if the owner has let the insurance lapse. Premiums for lender-placed, or forced-place, insurance are considerably higher than those for insurance an owner would buy. The coverage is also typically much less and limited to the structure itself. The lender will usually add the amount of the premium payment to the mortgage payments and require the homeowner to pay the higher amount. The lender will do this until the homeowner obtains a policy on his or her own.

Owner-placed insurance. A property owner should consider the following when seeking homeowner's insurance coverage:

- the size and value of the property
- the potential for an increase or decrease in the property's value

- the value of the items contained in the home
- the age of the items in the home and how much depreciation will impact their coverage if they need replacing
- the area where the property is located and what weather conditions may threaten the home
- what type of structure is being insured
- whether the property is rented or owner occupied
- the lender's coverage requirements
- the cost and terms of the policy

Policy features and types of coverage

Policy content. The content of a policy explains in detail what is covered and to what extent. If the policy does not include a specific peril or threat, then a loss caused by that peril will not be covered. For example, if the property is located in Florida, where hurricanes are prevalent, but a policy does not include coverage for hurricanes, then the homeowner will be responsible for repairing damage to the home caused by a hurricane. The same is true for mold. Many homeowner's policies specifically exclude coverage for mold. Therefore, if mold is discovered in the home, the insurance policy will not cover the cost of remediating the mold or for the loss of the use of the home while the mold is being remediated.

Declarations. The declarations page includes the basic details of the policy, effective dates, deductibles, endorsements, and the name of any mortgagee. It also states the insurance rating of the property as determined by the property description.

Each policy contains certain types of coverage. The coverages can be basic or comprehensive, providing more extensive coverage. The main types of coverage and those most commonly included in homeowners' policies are as follows.

Dwelling coverage. This pays for damage to the home itself and any structures or fixtures attached to the home. Coverage would include attached garages, plumbing, electrical systems, HVAC systems, and so forth. This is the most basic and common coverage and typically includes fire, windstorm, hail, tornadoes, vandalism, smoke, etc. It may not cover hurricanes, earthquakes, or mold unless specifically added.

Other structures coverage. This pays for damage to structures not attached to the home. These include unattached garages, fences, sheds, pool houses, or any other structure located on the property but not attached to the home.

Personal property coverage. This pays for the loss of personal belongings that are not considered to be the home itself. Examples include furniture, appliances, clothing, computers, televisions, home décor, books, and so forth. This coverage typically includes damage, loss, and theft of the personal property, whether or not it is actually on the property. For example, if the homeowner is traveling and loses a laptop computer during the trip, the personal property coverage on the owner's policy would pay for the laptop.

Loss of use coverage. This pays some expenses to live elsewhere after the home has been damaged or destroyed by a covered peril. Again, if the peril is not covered, the policy will not pay for loss of use. If there is no earthquake coverage under the policy and a home in California is damaged by an earthquake, the policy holder will not receive loss of use payment while the home is being repaired.

Liability coverage. This pays if the homeowner is sued and found to be responsible for someone being injured on the owner's property. If the stairs leading up to a home are covered with ice and the homeowner has not cleared the stairs, the owner might be held responsible for a visitor's injuries from a fall on the stairs. Liability insurance would cover the financial penalty imposed by the injured visitor's lawsuit. Liability also covers damage to someone else's property caused by the policyholder's negligence.

Medical payment coverage. This pays the medical bills if someone is hurt on the homeowner's property. When that same visitor slips on the icy stairs and is injured, the medical payment coverage would pay for the visitor's hospital and medical bills related to the fall. Also, if the homeowner owns a dog that injures someone, the medical payments coverage would pay for the resulting medical bills. However, some insurance companies exclude dogs altogether or exclude certain breeds of dogs that they deem to be dangerous breeds. In this case, if the policy excluded pit bulls and it was the homeowner's pit bull which bit someone, the policy would not pay for those medical bills.

Exclusions. It is worth mentioning again that numerous perils are typically excluded. These include hurricanes, earthquakes, and mold. However, for an increased premium, these perils can be added to the policy. Some types of coverage are always excluded from homeowners' policies, for example, flood. Separate flood policies are purchased through federal insurance programs.

Endorsements. An endorsement (or rider) provides coverage for property or perils not covered in the original policy. An example of an endorsement would be coverage for expensive jewelry.

Conditions. A condition is a specific requirement for coverage in a policy. For example, a car may be covered only when it is parked in the garage.

The 80% rule.

Homeowner policies should insure the home for at least 80% of the home's replacement cost. With this coverage, the insurance company will pay losses in full up to the face amount of the policy, minus the deductible. For example, if the total coverage amount is $300,000 and the deductible is $500, a total loss of the home would pay $299,500.

However, if the home is not insured for 80% of the replacement cost, the loss would be paid based on the actual cash value of the property. This coverage amount would be based on depreciation and the home's age. For example, the recovery from a total loss of the same $300,000 home may be considerably less than the cost to replace the home if the home is 10 years old. A 10-year depreciation amount would be figured into the loss, and the company would pay the loss based on that factor.

Deductibles

Most policies include a deductible, which is a stated amount of money the policy holder must pay before the insurance benefits commence. The deductible amount will be determined by the premium amount – the lower the deductible, the higher the premium. The typical deductible on a homeowner's policy is $500 to $1,000.

Renter's insurance

Individuals renting or leasing an apartment or a house may carry a renters' insurance policy. This policy will pay for damage or loss of the renter's personal property by any peril covered in the policy. Renters' insurance is similar to homeowners' insurance except it does not cover the actual dwelling. The landlord still needs to carry homeowners' insurance to cover the dwelling itself.

Types of homeowner policies

The HO-1 policy. HO-1 is the basis for most homeowners' policies. It provides coverage for losses from the following perils:

- theft
- lightning, wind, and hail
- fire and smoke
- theft and vandalism
- explosion
- civil damage and riots
- war and terrorism
- damage from vehicles and aircraft
- glass breakage
- damage to property being removed in an emergency situation such as fire

In addition, the HO-1 policy includes liability coverage for

- personal injury – resulting from negligence on the part of the insured
- medical payments – for injuries occurring to guests or resident employees of the insured
- physical damage – caused by the insured to the property of others

The HO-2 policy. HO-2, also known as a peril policy, covers items in addition to those included in the HO-1 policy. These items include electric current, accidental discharge of water, weight of ice and snow, falling objects and building collapse. In a peril policy, if the item is not listed, it is not covered.

The HO-3 policy. HO-3 is a more comprehensive all-risk policy that differs from the HO-2 in that it covers all perils unless they are listed in the policy.

The HO-4 policy. HO-4 is a policy is for renters. This policy covers personal property and liability for damage to the property or injuries to other people in the rented unit.

The HO-5 policy. HO-5 policies have the most comprehensive coverage of all the homeowners' policies. It includes coverage for structures, personal property and loss of use.

The HO-6 policy. HO-6 policies are specific to condominiums and cooperatives. This policy type does not cover the structure itself but does cover semi-permanent structures such as cabinets, carpeting, wallpaper, etc. It also covers personal property. The condominium association or cooperative would carry coverage for the actual structure.

The HO-7 policy. HO-7 policies provide an extended form of real and personal property coverage designed specifically for very expensive houses.

The HO-8 policy. HO-8 policies are for older homes with replacement costs higher than the home's market value. This policy type pays to repair or replace damaged property with cheaper common construction materials and methods, referred to as functional replacement.

FLOOD INSURANCE

FEMA & NFIP

The Federal Emergency Management Agency (FEMA) administers the National Flood Insurance Program (NFIP). The purpose of the NFIP is to reduce the financial impact of flooding on both private and public structures. In addition to providing affordable flood insurance, it also encourages the development of floodplain management regulations as well as their enforcement.

Flood zones

Flood zones as designated by FEMA are areas that border rivers and streams where flooding is a concern. Designated flood hazard zones are subject to restrictions on the location, type, and elevation of all improvements to the land (residential, agricultural, commercial, and industrial). Flood maps generally show a community's flood zones, floodplain boundaries, and Base Flood Elevation. This information, when examined together, determines the risk of flooding.

Flood hazards will change over time. The flow of water and how it drains can change due to natural or manmade causes. New land use and community development, natural forces such as climate change, terrain changes, and wildfires all can impact the risk of flooding.

To better reflect the current flood risk conditions, FEMA uses the latest technology to update and issue new flood maps nationwide to aid communities, property owners, businesses, and other stakeholders in taking steps to address flood risks. For informative videos and more information including flood maps, visit www.fema.gov and www.floodsmart.gov.

Flood insurance requirement

If a property is in a FEMA-designated flood hazard area, and financing is being obtained through a federally regulated mortgage loan, flood insurance is required. Flood insurance, which is a separate policy, cannot be purchased directly from the NFIP but must be purchased through the same companies that provide regular homeowners' insurance.

If an entire structure is above the 100-year flood plain, it has a 1% annual chance of flooding, and the requirement for flood insurance may be waived. The zone it is located in is called the Special Flood Hazard Area (SFHA), also known as the 1% annual chance flood zone. Properties located in low- to moderate-risk flood hazard areas such as the SFHA are not federally mandated to be covered by flood insurance; however, a lender may still require it. As flood hazard area maps are revised and properties move from low- to high-risk areas, flood insurance becomes a requirement.

Residents in a high-risk flood zone who have received federal disaster assistance in the form of grants from FEMA or low-interest disaster loans from the U.S. Small Business Administration (SBA) following a Presidential Disaster Declaration must maintain flood insurance in order to be considered for any future federal disaster aid.

Disclosure

Where applicable, licensees have the responsibility to disclose if any portion of a property is located in a flood hazard area, as this is a material fact. Buyers should be advised to consult FEMA flood maps and/or check with the local planning office to determine the precise location of any flood zones and restrictions.

PROPERTY INSURABILITY

Determining the insurability of a property should always be part of a purchaser's due diligence process, and brokers should advise clients accordingly.

If a purchaser has a large claims history, obtaining insurance may be difficult, or premiums may be very expensive, as companies try to mitigate their risk. Claims that attract particular attention include slips and falls, water damage, and dog bites. Companies commonly keep a list of the dogs most likely to bite as determined by the Centers for Disease Control and Prevention. Owning a dog on the CDC's list can make it difficult to obtain coverage. Higher premiums can also be expected in high risk areas such as those prone to hurricanes or fire.

CLUE reports

Insurance companies are required to report all claims for which they set up a file for a possible claim, deny a claim, or pay out money for a claim. The consumer reporting agency LexisNexis compiles claim report files and generates Comprehensive Loss Underwriting Exchange (CLUE) reports.

A CLUE report goes back for up to seven years, listing both personal property and personal auto claims, and includes the following information:

- name
- date of birth
- policy number
- date of loss
- type of loss
- description of covered property
- amount paid out by the insurance company
- property address (for property claims) or vehicle information (for auto claims)

INSURING VACANT AND UNOCCUPIED PROPERTY

Brokers may encounter transactions where a property is or has been vacant for a period of time, a buyer wants to take possession before closing, or a seller wants to continue possession for a time after closing. All of these situations carry specific insurance concerns. Brokers should advise sellers to maintain coverage until after closing as the Risk of Loss remains the responsibility of the seller.

Vacant property

Vacant property is not inhabited and does not contain the personal property needed to support occupancy. Vacant properties carry a higher risk for vandalism and damage that goes undiscovered for an extended period of time. Homeowners' policies typically contain vacancy exclusions that include water damage, theft, vandalism, and glass breakage if the property has been vacant and the damage occurs within 30-60 days of becoming vacant (the exact terms depend on state law and the type of policy).

A vacant home is more difficult and expensive to insure; however, no property should ever go without coverage, so owners are advised to discuss obtaining a vacancy policy with their insurance provider. When available, vacant home coverage can be three times more expensive than the coverage for an occupied home.

Unoccupied property

Unoccupied property is different from vacant property. An unoccupied property is one that still contains all the furnishings needed so the owner could return at any time. Unoccupied properties are often vacation homes where the owner spends significant time away from the property. In this situation, the home may still be covered under the normal homeowners' policy. Owners should consult with their insurance provider to determine whether their policy excludes unoccupied building coverage and prevents the recovery of damages if the property is vacant for more than 60 consecutive days.

Vacant commercial property

A commercial property must have at least 31% of its total square footage occupied to avoid being considered vacant. Like homeowners' policies, commercial policies exclude coverage for water damage, theft, and vandalism when a property has been vacant for 60 days. In addition, commercial policies typically reduce coverage for perils by 15% when the property is vacant.

Early or late possession

For many reasons, early or late possession are tricky situations for all buyers, sellers, and brokers. Brokers are reminded to use the appropriate addenda for these situations and to advise their clients to confirm coverage for their particular situation with their insurance provider ahead of time.

For early possession by the buyer, the seller will most likely need to obtain a landlord's policy, as homeowners' policies typically do not cover the home if it is not owner occupied. Buyers assuming possession early are advised to purchase renters' insurance to cover their personal property and to obtain regular homeowners' coverage beginning on the day of closing.

==

SNAPSHOT REVIEW: UNIT TEN

HOMEOWNERS INSURANCE AND FLOOD INSURANCE

PURPOSE

- Protect asset against possible loss- flood, auto, health, business, life or pets
- Common insurance-homeowners' insurance, flood insurance

HOMEOWNERS INSURANCE ESSENTIALS

Lender-placed v owner-placed insurance
- Most lenders will place homeowner's insurance on home if owner has let insurance lapse
- Lender-placed insurance premiums higher than those owner would incur

Policy features and types of coverage
- Policy explains in detail what is covered
- If policy does not include specific peril or threat, then loss will not be covered
- Dwelling coverage - damage to home and structures or fixtures attached to home
- Other structures coverage - damage to structures not attached to home
- Personal property coverage - loss of personal belongings not considered to be home itself
- Loss of use coverage - expenses to live elsewhere after home damaged
- Liability coverage - if homeowner sued and found to be responsible for someone being injured
- Medical payment coverage - medical bills if someone hurt on homeowner's property
- Numerous perils typically excluded - hurricanes, earthquakes, and mold. Can be added to policy for increased premium

The 80% rule
- Insure home for at least 80% of home's replacement cost

Deductibles
- Amount of money policy holder must pay before insurance benefits commence

Renter's insurance
- Will pay for damage or loss of renter's personal property by any peril covered in the policy

Types of homeowner policies
- HO-1 policy: basis for most homeowners' policies. Coverage for theft, fire, explosion, war, personal injury, etc.
- HO-2 policy: peril policy. Covers items in addition to those in HO-1 policy
- HO-3 policy: all-risk policy. Covers all perils unless listed in policy
- HO-4 policy: for renters. Covers personal property and liability for damage to property or injuries to other people in rented unit
- HO-5 policy: most comprehensive coverage of all homeowners' policies. Coverage for structures, personal property and loss of use
- HO-6 policy: specific to condominiums and cooperatives
- HO-7 policy: extended real and personal property coverage designed for expensive houses
  HO-8 policy: older homes with replacement costs higher than home's market value

FLOOD INSURANCE

FEMA & NFIP
- Federal Emergency Management Agency administers National Flood Insurance Program
- NFIP purpose to reduce financial impact of flooding on private and public structures

Flood zones
- Designated by FEMA
- Border rivers and streams where flooding is concern

Flood insurance requirement
- If property in FEMA-designated flood hazard area, and financing through a federally regulated mortgage loan, flood insurance required

Disclosure
- Licensees have the responsibility to disclose if any portion of a property is located in a flood hazard area

PROPERTY INSURABILITY

- Determining insurability of property should be part of purchaser's due diligence process, and brokers should advise clients accordingly

CLUE reports
- Consumer reporting agency LexisNexis compiles claim report files and generates Comprehensive Loss Underwriting Exchange reports
- CLUE reports go back for up to 7 years, listing both personal property and personal auto claims

INSURING VACANT AND UNOCCUPIED PROPERTY

Vacant property
- Not inhabited. Does not contain personal property needed to support occupancy
- Carries higher risk for vandalism and damage
- More difficult and expensive to insure

Unoccupied property
- Contains furnishings needed so owner could return at any time (vacation homes, etc)
- Might still be covered under normal homeowners' policy

Vacant commercial property
- Must have at least 31% of its total square footage occupied to avoid being considered vacant

Early or late possession
- For early possession by buyer, seller most likely need to obtain a landlord's policy
- Buyers assuming possession early advised to purchase renter's insurance to cover personal property

===

Check Your Understanding Quiz:

Unit Ten: Homeowners Insurance and Flood Insurance

Carefully read each question then provide your best answer based on what you learned in this unit. Then check your answers against the Answer Key which immediately follows the quiz questions.

1. Insurance premiums for _____ insurance are considerably higher than those an owner would buy.

    a. title-placed
    b. lender-placed
    c. agent-based
    d. buyer-placed

2. Which insurance coverage would include attached garages?

    a. Dwelling coverage
    b. Structures coverage
    c. Loss of use coverage
    d. Liability coverage

3. Homeowner insurance policies should insure the home for at least _____ of the home's replacement cost.

    a. 80%
    b. 50%
    c. 75%
    d. 25%

4. Which insurance policy is specific to condominiums?

    a. HO-2 policy
    b. HO-4 policy
    c. HO-6 policy
    d. HO-8 policy

5. CLUE reports list both personal property and personal _____ claims.

    a. health
    b. travel
    c. finance
    d. auto

6. Andrew's roof was damaged by a hurricane, so he had to stay at a nearby hotel while it was replaced. What type of insurance coverage will cover his hotel stay?

    a. Personal property coverage
    b. Loss of use coverage
    c. Disaster coverage
    d. Liability coverage

===

Answer Key:

Unit Ten: Homeowners Insurance and Flood Insurance

1. **b. lender-placed**

2. **a. Dwelling coverage**

3. **a. 80%**

4. **c. HO-6 policy**

5. **d. auto**

6. **b. Loss of use coverage**

UNIT 11:

REAL ESTATE ECONOMICS AND VALUATION

Unit Eleven Learning Objectives: When the student has completed this unit he or she will be able to:

- Identify the key correlations between real estate supply, demand and prices and how market influences can affect their interaction.
- Summarize the essential determinants of value and the valuation laws underlying residential market valuation.
- Describe how the sales comparison approach to valuation works and how comparables form the basis for the estimate of value.
- Explain the income approach to value and the step-by-step process for deriving income property valuation estimates using the approach.

REAL ESTATE SUPPLY AND DEMAND

Supply

In real estate, supply is the amount of property available for sale or lease at any given time. The units of supply used to quantify the amount of property available differ for different categories of property. These supply units, by property type, are:

- residential real estate: dwelling units
- commercial and industrial real estate: square feet
- agricultural property: acreage

Factors influencing supply. In addition to the influences of demand, real estate supply responds to

- development costs, particularly labor
- availability of financing
- investment returns
- a community's master plan
- government police powers and regulation

Demand

Real estate demand is the amount of property buyers and tenants wish to acquire by purchase, lease or trade at any given time. Units of demand, by property classification, are:

- residential: households
- commercial and industrial: square feet
- agricultural: acreage

The unit of residential demand is the household, which is an individual or family who would occupy a dwelling unit. Residential demand can be further broken down into demand to lease versus buy, and demand for single family homes versus apartments.

Residential demand can be very difficult to quantify. One measure is the number of buyers employing agents to locate property. Another measure is the net population change in an area, plus families that attempted to move in but could not.

Factors affecting demand. The demand for particular types of real estate relates to the specific concerns of users. These concerns revolve around the components of value: desire, utility, scarcity, and purchasing power.

Residential users are concerned with:

- quality of life
- neighborhood quality
- convenience and access to services and other facilities
- dwelling amenities in relation to household size, lifestyle, and costs

Retail users are concerned with:

- sufficient trade area population and income
- the level of trade area competition
- sales volume per square foot of rented area
- consumer spending patterns
- growth patterns in the trade area

Office users are concerned with:

costs of occupancy to the business

- efficiency of the building and the suite in accommodating the business's functions
- accessibility by employees and suppliers
- matching building quality to the image and function of the business

Industrial users are concerned with:

- functionality
- the availability and proximity of the labor pool
- compliance with environmental regulations
- permissible zoning
- health and safety of the workers
- access to suppliers and distribution channels

Market influences on supply and demand

Numerous factors in a market influence the real estate cycle to speed up or slow down. These influences can be local or national, and from the public or private economic sector.

Local market influences. Since the real estate market is local by definition, local factors weigh heavily in local real estate market conditions. Among these are:

- cost of financing
- availability of developable land
- construction costs
- capacity of the municipality's infrastructure to handle growth
- governmental regulation and police powers
- changes in the economic base
- in- and out-migrations of major employers

National trends. Regional and national economic forces influence the local real estate market in the form of:

- changes in money supply
- inflation
- national economic cycles

In recent years international economic trends have increasingly influenced local real estate markets, particularly in border states, large metropolitan areas, and in markets where the economic base is tied to foreign trade. In these instances, currency fluctuations have significant impact on the local economy.

Governmental influences. Governments at every level exert significant influence over local real estate markets. The primary forms of government influence are:

- local zoning power
- local control and permitting of new development
- local taxing power
- federal influence on interest rates
- environmental legislation and regulations

A good example of government influence over the local real estate market is a city government's power to declare a moratorium on new construction, regardless of demand. Such officially declared stoppages may occur because of water or power shortages, insufficiency of thoroughfares, or incompatibility with the master plan

UNDERLYING DETERMINANTS OF VALUE

Price is not something of value in itself. It is only a number that quantifies value. The economic issue underlying the interplay of supply and demand is, how do trading parties arrive at the value of a product or service as indicated by the price?

The value of something is based on the answers to four questions:

- How much do I desire it?
- How useful is it?
- How scarce is it?
- Am I able to pay for it?

Desire

One determinant of value is how dear the item is to the purchaser. Assume a person is considering buying an air conditioner. Here, the question becomes "how much do I desire to be cool, dry, and comfortable?" To a person who lives in Florida, it is safe to say that air conditioning is more valuable than a heating system. It is also safe to say the opposite is true for residents of northern Alaska.

Utility

The second determinant of value is the product's ability to do the job, or utility. Can the air conditioner satisfy my need to stay cool? How cool does it make my house? Does it even work properly? Of course, I won't pay as much if it is old or ineffectual.

Scarcity

The third critical element of value is a product's availability in relation to demand. The air conditioner is quite valuable if there are only five units in the entire city and everyone is hot. On the other hand, the value of an air conditioner goes down if there are ten thousand units for sale in a 500-person market.

Affordability

The fourth component of value is the consumer's ability to pay for the item, or its affordability. If one cannot afford to buy the air conditioner, the value of the air conditioner is diminished, since it is financially out of reach. If all air conditioners are too expensive, consumers are forced to consider alternatives such as ceiling fans.

In the marketplace, the relative presence or absence of the four determinants of value is constantly changing due to supply and demand factors. Since price is a reflection of the total of all value factors at any time, changes in the underlying factors of value trigger changes in price.

PRINCIPLES OF VALUE

A number of economic forces interact in the marketplace to contribute to real estate value. Real estate professionals must consider these forces in estimating the value of a property either for a broker's opinion of value or for a full-blown appraisal. For residential properties, the primary principles of value are supply and demand (previously discussed), substitution and contribution. For income properties, the principle of anticipation comes into play.

Substitution

According to the principle of substitution, a buyer will pay no more for a property than the buyer would have to pay for an equally desirable and available substitute property. For example, if three houses for sale are essentially similar in size, quality and location, a potential buyer is unlikely to choose the one that is priced significantly higher than the other two. This principle underlies the Competitive Market Analysis, or CMA – since buyer will pay similar amounts for similar properties, the analyst's first step is to identify similar properties and what they recently sold for.

Contribution

Contribution. The principle of contribution focuses on *the degree to which a particular improvement affects the market value of the overall property*. In essence, the contribution of the improvement is equal to the change in market value that the addition of the improvement causes. For example, adding a bathroom to a house may contribute an additional $15,000 to the appraised value. Thus the contribution of the bathroom is $15,000. Note that an improvement's contribution to value has little to do with the improvement's cost. The foregoing bathroom may have cost $5,000 or $20,000. Contribution is what the market recognizes as the change in value, not what an item cost.

Anticipation

The income benefits a buyer expects to derive from a property over a holding period largely determines what the buyer is willing to pay for it. For example, if an investor anticipates an annual rental income from a leased property to be one million dollars, this expected sum has a direct bearing on what the investor will pay for the property. This amount will then complete the picture of the investor's return as a percent of the investment amount.

DEFINING MARKET VALUE

Market value is an opinion of the price that a willing seller and willing buyer would probably agree on for a property at a given time if:

- the transaction is a cash transaction
- the property is exposed on the open market for a reasonable period
- buyer and seller have full information about market conditions and about potential uses
- there is no abnormal pressure on either party to complete the transaction
- buyer and seller are not related (it is an "arm's length" transaction)
- title is marketable and conveyable by the seller
- the price is a "normal consideration," that is, it does not include hidden influences such as special financing deals, concessions, terms, services, fees, credits, costs, or other types of consideration.

Another way of describing market value is that it is the highest price that a buyer would pay and the lowest price that the seller would accept for the property.

Price vs. value

The market price, as opposed to market value, is what a property actually sells for. Market price should theoretically be the same as market value if all the conditions essential for market value were present. Market price, however, may not reflect the analysis of comparables and of investment value that an estimate of market value includes.

Broker's opinion of value (BPO)

A broker's opinion of value may resemble an appraisal, but it differs from an appraisal in that it is not necessarily performed by a disinterested third party or licensed professional. In addition, the BPO generally uses only a limited form of one of the three appraisal approaches, namely the sales comparison approach. Finally, the opinion is not subject to regulation, nor does it follow any particular professional standards as promulgated by appraisal regulators.

THE SALES COMPARISON APPROACH

The sales comparison approach, also known as the market data approach, is used for almost all properties. It also serves as the basis for a broker's opinion of value. It is based on the principle of substitution-- that a buyer will pay no more for the subject property than would be sufficient to purchase a comparable property-- and contribution-- that specific characteristics add value to a property.

The sales comparison approach is widely used because it takes into account the subject property's specific amenities in relation to competing properties. In addition, because of the currency of its data, the approach incorporates present market realities.

Steps in the approach

- Identify comparable sales.
- Compare comparables to the subject and make adjustments to comparables.
- Weight values indicated by adjusted comparables for the final value estimate of the subject.

The sales comparison approach consists of comparing sale prices of recently sold properties that are comparable with the subject, and making dollar adjustments to the price of each comparable to account for competitive differences with the subject. After identifying the adjusted value of each comparable, the appraiser weights the reliability of each comparable and the factors underlying how the adjustments were made. The weighting yields a final value range based on the most reliable factors in the analysis.

Identifying comparables

To qualify as a comparable, a property must:

- resemble the subject in size, shape, design, utility and location
- have sold recently, generally within six months of the appraisal
- have sold in an arm's-length transaction

To complete the analysis, the appraiser will consider three to six comparables. Preferably the chosen comps are as similar to each other as possible and have sold as recently as possible.

Adjusting comparables

The appraiser adjusts the sale prices of the comparables to account for competitive differences with the subject property. Note that the sale prices of the comparables are known, while the value and price of the subject are not. Therefore, adjustments can be made only to the comparables' prices, not to the subject's. Adjustments are made to the comparables in the form of a value deduction or a value addition.

Adding or deducting value. If the comparable is better than the subject in some characteristic, an amount is *deducted* from the sale price of the comparable. This effectively accounts for the comparable's value difference in an adjustment category.

For example, a comparable has a swimming pool and the subject does not. To equalize the difference, the appraiser *deducts* an amount, say $6,000, from the sale price of the comparable. Note that the adjustment reflects the *contribution of the swimming pool to market value*. The adjustment amount is not the cost of the pool or its depreciated value.

If the comparable is inferior to the subject in some characteristic, an amount is *added* to the price of the comparable. This adjustment equalizes the subject's competitive advantage in this area.

Adjustment criteria. The principal factors for comparison and adjustment are time of sale, location, physical characteristics, and transaction characteristics.

- **time of sale**

  An adjustment may be made if market conditions, market prices, or financing availability have changed significantly since the date of the comparable's sale. Most often, this adjustment is to account for appreciation.

- **location**

  An adjustment may be made if there are differences between the comparable's location and the subject's, including neighborhood desirability and appearance, zoning restrictions, and general price levels.

- **physical characteristics**

  Adjustments may be made for marketable differences between the comparable's and subject's lot size, square feet of livable area (or other appropriate measure for the property type), number of rooms, layout, age, condition, construction type and quality, landscaping, and special amenities.

- **transaction characteristics**

  An adjustment may be made for such differences as mortgage loan terms, mortgage assumability, and owner financing.

Weighting comps and the final estimate

Adding and subtracting the appropriate adjustments to the sale price of each comparable results in an adjusted price for the comparables that indicates the value of the subject. The last step in the approach is to perform a weighted analysis of the indicated values of each comparable. In other words, one must identify which comparable values are more indicative of the subject and which are less indicative.

There is no formula for selecting a value from within the range of all comparables analyzed. However, there are three quantitative guidelines: the *total number* of adjustments; the *amount of a single adjustment*; and the *net value change* of all adjustments.

As a rule, the fewer the total number of adjustments, the smaller the adjustment amounts, and the less the total adjustment amount, the more reliable the comparable.

Number of adjustments. In terms of total adjustments, the comparable with the fewest adjustments tends to be most similar to the subject, hence the best indicator of value. If a comparable requires excessive adjustments, it is increasingly less reliable as an indicator of value.

Single adjustment amounts. The dollar amount of an adjustment represents the variance between the subject and the comparable for a given item. If a large adjustment is called for, the comparable becomes less of an indicator of value. The smaller the adjustment, the better the comparable is as an indicator of value.

Total net adjustment amount. The third reliability factor in weighting comparables is the total net value change of all adjustments added together. If a comparable's total adjustments alter the indicated value only slightly, the comparable is a good indicator of value. If total adjustments create a large dollar amount between the sale price and the adjusted value, the comparable is a poorer indicator of value.

THE INCOME APPROACH

The income capitalization approach, or income approach, is used for income properties and sometimes for other properties in a rental market where the appraiser can find rental data. The approach is based on the principle of anticipation: the expected future income stream of a property underlies what an investor will pay for the property. It is also based on the principle of substitution: that an investor will pay no more for a subject property with a certain income stream than the investor would have to pay for another property with a similar income stream.

Steps in the approach

The income capitalization method consists of estimating annual net operating income from the subject property, then applying a capitalization rate to the income. This produces a principal amount that the investor would pay for the property.

Steps in the Income Approach

1. Estimate potential gross income.
2. Estimate effective gross income.
3. Estimate net operating income.
4. Select a capitalization rate.
5. Apply the capitalization rate.

Estimate potential gross income. Potential gross income is the scheduled rent of the subject plus income from miscellaneous sources such as vending machines and telephones. Scheduled rent is the total rent a property will produce if fully leased at the established rental rates.

Scheduled rent

+ Other income

= Potential gross income

Estimate effective gross income. Effective gross income is potential gross income minus an allowance for vacancy and credit losses.

Potential gross income

- Vacancy & credit losses

= Effective gross income

The allowance for vacancy and credit loss is usually estimated as a percentage of potential gross income.

Estimate net operating income (NOI). Net operating income is effective gross income minus total operating expenses.

Effective gross income

- Total operating expenses

= Net operating income

Operating expenses include real estate taxes, hazard insurance, utilities, janitorial service, management, and repairs. Operating expenses do not include debt service, expenditures for capital improvements, or expenses not related to operation of the property.

Select and apply a capitalization rate. The capitalization rate is an estimate of the rate of return an investor will demand on the investment of capital in a property such as the subject. This is similar to the interest rate on a CD. It is synonymous with investment yield. Once selected, the appraiser must apply it to net income to derive value. This is done by dividing the estimated net operating income for the subject by the selected capitalization rate

Net operating income

÷ Capitalization rate

= Value estimate

INCOME APPROACH ILLUSTRATION

I. ESTIMATE POTENTIAL GROSS INCOME

Potential gross rental income	192,000
Plus: other income	2,000
Potential gross income	194,000

II. ESTIMATE EFFECTIVE GROSS INCOME

Less: vacancy and collection losses	9,600
Effective gross income	184,400

III. ESTIMATE NET OPERATING INCOME

Operating expenses	
Real estate taxes	32,000
Insurance	4,400
Utilities	12,000
Repairs	4,000
Maintenance	16,000
Management	12,000
Reserves	1,600
Legal and accounting	2,000
Total expenses	84,000
Effective gross income	184,400
Less: total expenses	84,000
Net operating income	100,400

Net operating income: $100,400

÷ Capitalization rate: 10% or .10

= Value estimate: $1,004,000

===

SNAPSHOT REVIEW: UNIT ELEVEN

REAL ESTATE ECONOMICS AND VALUATION

REAL ESTATE SUPPLY AND DEMAND

Supply
- Amount of property available for sale or lease
- Influenced by development costs, availability of financing, investment returns, community's master plan, government police powers. regulation

Demand
- Amount of property buyers and tenants wish to acquire by purchase, lease or trade
- Affected by quality of life, neighborhood, functionality, and permissible zoning

Market influences on supply and demand
- Local market influences-cost of financing, availability of developable land, changes in economic base, etc.
- National market influences- changes in money supply, inflation, and national economic cycles Government influences- local zoning power, local taxing power, environmental legislation and regulations, etc.

UNDERLYING DETERMINANTS OF VALUE

- Price is not something of value in itself

Desire
- How dear is item to purchaser?

Utility
- What is product's ability to do job?

Scarcity
- What is product's availability in relation to demand?

Affordability
- What is consumer's ability to pay for item?

PRINCIPLES OF VALUE

- Economic forces interact in marketplace contribute to real estate value

Substitution
- Buyer will pay no more for a property than would have to pay for an equally desirable and available substitute property
- Underlies the Competitive Market Analysis (CMA)

Contribution
- Focuses on degree to which particular improvement affects market value of overall property

Anticipation
- Income benefits buyer expects to derive from property over holding period largely determines what buyer is willing to pay for it

DEFINING MARKET VALUE

- A quantity of value that willing seller and willing buyer would probably agree on for property
- Highest price that buyer would pay and lowest price that seller would accept for property

Price vs. value

- Market price is what property actually sells for
- Market price should theoretically be same as market value if all conditions essential for market value were present

Broker's opinion of value (BPO)

- Uses a limited form of one of three appraisal approaches, especially sales comparison approach
- Not subject to regulation
- Does not follow any particular professional standards as promulgated by appraisal regulators

THE SALES COMPARISON APPROACH

- Known as market data approach
- Based on principle of substitution
- Incorporates market realities

Steps in the approach

- Identify comparable sales
- Compare comparables to subject and make adjustments to comparables
- Weight values indicated by adjusted comparables for final value estimate of subject

Identifying comparables

- Must be similar to subject in size, shape, design, utility and location
- Must have sold recently, generally within six months of appraisal
- Must have sold in an arm's-length transaction

Adjusting comparables

- Appraiser adjusts sale prices of comparables to account for differences with subject property
- Sales prices of comparables are known, while value and price of subject are not
- Adjustments are made only to comparables' values as a deduction or addition
- Primary adjustment criteria include time of sale, location, physical characteristics, and transaction characteristics

Weighting comps and the final estimate

- One must identify which comparable values are more indicative of subject
- The fewer the total number of adjustments, the smaller the adjustment amounts, and the less the total adjustment amount, the more reliable the comparable

THE INCOME APPROACH

- Used for income properties and sometimes for other properties in a rental market where appraiser can find rental data
- Based on principal of anticipation and principal of substitution

Steps in the approach

- Estimate potential gross income; estimate effective gross income; estimate net operating income; select capitalization rate; apply capitalization rate

Check Your Understanding Quiz:

Unit Eleven: Real Estate Economics and Valuation

Carefully read each question then provide your best answer based on what you learned in this unit. Then check your answers against the Answer Key which immediately follows the quiz questions.

1. Which of the following is a factor influencing supply?

    a. Quality of life
    b. Neighborhood quality
    c. Development costs
    d. Growth patterns in the area

2. Which of the following is a determinant of value?

    a. Desire
    b. Substitution
    c. Contribution
    d. Anticipation

3. The principle of _____ focuses on the degree to which a particular improvement affects the market value of the overall property.

    a. anticipation
    b. contribution
    c. substitution
    d. scarcity

4. What is the first step in the sales comparison approach?

    a. Identifying comparable sales
    b. Making adjustments to the comparable properties
    c. Comparing comparable properties to the subject
    d. Weighing the values indicated by the adjustments

5. Which method consists of estimating annual net operating income from the subject property?

    a. Sales comparison method
    b. Market data method
    c. Cost method
    d. Income capitalization method

6. _____ differs from an appraisal because it is not necessarily performed by a licensed professional.

   a. Comparison valuation
   b. Capitalization valuation
   c. Broker's opinion of value
   d. Licensee's opinion of value

===

Answer Key:

Unit Eleven: Real Estate Economics and Valuation

1. **c. Development costs**

2. **a. Desire**

3. **b. contribution**

4. **a. Identifying comparable sales**

5. **d. Income capitalization method**

6. **c. Broker's opinion of value**

UNIT 12:

ANALYSIS OF CAPITAL GAIN AND CASH FLOW

Unit Twelve Learning Objectives: When the student has completed this unit he or she will be able to:

- Define key capital gain and cash flow analysis terms and describe the specific steps involved in deriving the capital gain or loss of a residential or income property.
- Describe the steps involved in deriving pre-tax cash flow of an income property.
- Explain how investors derive tax liability from an investment property.
- Summarize how to derive after-tax cash flow using pre-tax cash flow and tax liability.
- Explain how a cash flow analysis can be used by investors to evaluate the desirability or feasibility of a given investment.

KEY TERMS

Depreciation. Cost recovery, or depreciation, allows the owner of income property to deduct a portion of the property's value from gross income each year over the life of the asset. The "life of the asset" and the deductible portion are defined by law. The amount of deductible value is the value of the property minus the land. When the property is acquired, this amount is the **beginning basis**. When periodic amounts of the improvement value are depreciated, the depreciable basis is lowered by such amount.

Basis and depreciable basis. Basis is the cost of a capital asset at a point in time. In real estate, the basis of a property is both the value of the land and any improvements. Since the land portion of the real property is not depreciable, only the improvements acquired can be depreciated. The undepreciated improvement portion of the property is therefore the **depreciable basis**. As the property is depreciated, or new capital improvements are added, the basis is adjusted accordingly and becomes a new **adjusted basis**.

Capital improvement. An addition or significant repair to a property that augments the property's value. For tax purposes, capital improvement costs are added to the adjusted basis of the property as opposed to being expensed against income in the year the improvement is made. As an add-on to the property's basis, the improvement is then depreciated along with the rest of the property's depreciable basis. Examples of a capital improvement are a widened garage, a swimming pool, or an upgraded roof.

Capital gain / loss. When real estate, whether non-income or income, is sold, a taxable event occurs. If the sale proceeds to the seller exceed the original cost of the investment, subject to some adjustments, there is a capital gain that is subject to tax. If the sales proceeds are less than the original cost with adjustments, there is a capital loss.

Deductible expense. An expense incurred by an income property that was paid to keep the property operating and maintained is tax-deductible. This means the owner can deduct the expense against taxable rental income. This effectively lowers the income property's income tax liability. Be careful, however, not to confuse an income property's income tax liability with the property's capital gain tax liability. The latter is only incurred when the income property is sold. This taxable event triggers either a capital gain or capital loss.

Taxable income. Taxable income from investment real estate is the gross income received minus any expenses, deductions or exclusions that current tax law allows. Taxable income from real estate is added to the investor's other income and taxed at the investor's marginal tax rate.

CAPITAL GAIN ANALYSIS

The seller of real property may owe tax on capital gain that results from the sale. Capital gain applies to the sale of both residential and income properties. The gain on the sale of a property is equal to the amount realized from the sale minus the adjusted basis of the home sold. Therefore, to identify the capital gain that will be incurred, one must complete the following steps:

1. Identify the amount realized from the sale of the property
2. Identify the adjusted basis of the property
3. Subtract the adjusted basis from the amount realized to identify the capital gain.

Amount realized

The amount realized, also known as net proceeds from sale, is expressed by the formula:

> sale price
>
> - costs of sale
>
> = amount realized

The sale price is the total amount the seller receives for the home. This includes money, notes, mortgages or other debts the buyer assumes as part of the sale.

Costs of sale include brokerage commissions, relevant advertising, legal fees, seller-paid points and other closing costs. Certain fix-up expenses can be deducted from the amount realized to derive an adjusted sale price.

Adjusted basis

Basis is a measurement of how much is invested in the property for tax purposes. Assuming that the property was acquired through purchase, the beginning basis is the cost of acquiring the property. Cost includes cash and debt obligations, and such other settlement costs as legal and recording fees, abstract fees, surveys, charges for installing utilities, transfer taxes, title insurance, and any other amounts the buyer pays for the seller.

The beginning basis is increased or decreased by certain types of expenditures made while the property is owned. Basis is increased by the cost of capital improvements made to the property. Assessments for local improvements such as roads and sidewalks also increase the basis. Examples of capital improvements are: putting on an addition, paving a driveway, replacing a roof, adding central air conditioning, and rewiring the home.

The basic formula for adjusted basis is:

> beginning basis
>
> + capital improvements
>
> - depreciation
>
> = adjusted basis

Gain on sale

The gain on sale of a primary residence is represented by the basic formula:

> amount realized (net sales proceeds)
>
> - adjusted basis
>
> = gain on sale

Gain on sale, if it does not qualify for an exclusion under current tax law, is taxable.

Residential capital gain analysis illustration

The following items and amounts illustrate the derivation of the capital gain on a residential property.

Gain on Sale

	Selling price of old home	$350,000
-	Selling costs	35,000
=	Amount realized	315,000
	Beginning basis of old home	200,000
+	Capital improvements	10,000
=	Adjusted basis of old home	210,000
	Amount realized	315,000
-	Adjusted basis	210,000
=	Gain on sale	105,000

INCOME PROPERTY CASH FLOW ANALYSIS

Besides the capital gain analysis, the other principal type of financial analysis done on real property is the cash flow analysis. A cash flow analysis can be done on a pre-tax or an after-tax basis. The term cash flow is essentially the same as profit. The analysis simply consists of identifying income, expenses, pre-tax profit, tax liability, then after-tax profit.

Steps in the cash flow analysis

As stated, cash flow analysis of an income property amounts to the identification of the property's income, expenses, tax liability and net profit after tax. The specific steps are:

1. Identify the pre-tax cash flow
2. Identify the tax liability
3. Derive the after-tax cash flow

Investors will then use the after-tax profit number to evaluate a fair value, or price for the property. This will complete the investor's picture of the investment cost (price), the return (net income), and the return percent (yield percent).

Pre-tax cash flow

Cash flow is the difference between the amount of actual cash flowing into the investment as revenue and out of the investment for expenses, debt service, and all other items. Cash flow concerns cash items only, and therefore excludes depreciation, which is not a cash expense. Pre-tax cash flow, or cash flow before taxation, is calculated as follows:

Pre-tax Cash Flow

	potential rental income
-	vacancy and collection loss
=	effective rental income
+	other income
=	gross operating income
-	operating expenses
-	reserves
=	net operating income (NOI)
-	debt service
=	pre-tax cash flow

Potential rental income is the annual amount that would be realized if the property is fully leased or rented at the scheduled rate. Vacancy and collection loss is rental income lost because of vacancies or tenants' failure to pay rent.

Effective rental income is the potential income adjusted for these losses. To that is added any other income the property generates, such as from laundry or parking charges, to obtain gross operating income.

Operating expenses paid by the landlord include such items as utilities and maintenance. These are deducted from gross operating income. Some owners also set aside a cash reserve each year to build up a fund for capital replacements in the future, for example, to replace a roof or a furnace. Cash reserves are not deductible for tax purposes until spent as deductible repairs or maintenance.

The remainder is **net operating income** (NOI). When the annual amount paid for debt service, including principal and interest, is subtracted, the remainder is the pre-tax cash flow.

Tax liability

The owner's tax liability on taxable income from the property is based on taxable income rather than cash flow. Taxable income and tax liability, with an example, are calculated as follows:

Tax Liability

	net operating income (NOI)	29,300
+	reserves	3,500
-	interest expense	10,000
-	cost recovery expense	22,000
=	taxable income	800
x	tax rate (24%)	
=	tax liability	192

Taxable income is net operating income minus all allowable deductions. Cost recovery, or depreciation expense, is allowed as a deduction, while allowances for reserves and payments on loan principal payback are not allowed. Thus, since reserves were deducted from gross operating income to determine NOI, this amount must be added back in. As only the interest portion of debt service is deductible, the principal amount must be removed from the debt service payments and the interest expense deducted from NOI.

Finally, taxable income, multiplied by the owner's marginal tax bracket, reveals the tax liability.

After-tax cash flow

After-tax cash flow is the amount of income from the property that actually goes into the owner's pocket *after income tax is paid*. So the analyst must subtract tax liability from pre-tax cash flow. Continuing with the previous example, this is figured as:

After-tax Cash Flow

	pre-tax cash flow	9,300
-	tax liability	224
=	after-tax cash flow	9,076

Applying the analysis to investments

The cash flow analysis is essential for investors to understand the property's yield in relation to its value or price. Most investors have a sense for how much yield they require from a property given its various risk factors. Knowing cash flow enables the investor to establish a price range.   The formulas are:

1. **Price** = income ÷ rate of return
2. **Rate of return** = income ÷ price
3. **Income** = price x rate of return

These formulas are used to identify the three things an investor needs to evaluate an investment: price, rate of return, and income. The cash flow analysis is necessary to derive income.

Identifying price. Applying these formulas, let's assume that an investor's required yield on an income property is a minimum of 10% before tax. Now the investor knows that, if there is a property that produces $200,000 profit, then it must be priced at no more than $2 million in order for it to yield 10%.

By contrast, let's assume the same property yielding $200,000 is located in a deteriorating, transitioning neighborhood. Now the investor wants more yield because the investment is riskier. Let's assume the investor must now yield 15%. What must the price be for this? In other words, what number times 15% equals $200,000. Per the formula above that solves for price, the answer is $200,000 ÷ .15 (15%), or $1,333,333.

Identifying rate of return. Using the formula "rate of return = income ÷ price," the investor can use the cash flow analysis to evaluate the yield of varying properties on the market. Assume then a property is priced at $1.5 million, and the property yields a pre-tax cash flow of $95,000. What is the property's yield? Will our investor be interested if he or she must get a 10% yield? The answer using the formula is that the rate of return is $95,000 ÷ $1.5 million, or 6.3%. Should this investor buy this property at this price? Clearly not.

To summarize, knowing the cash flow of a property enables a prospective buyer to identify either the yield or required price of a given investment opportunity.

==

SNAPSHOT REVIEW: UNIT TWELVE

ANALYSIS OF CAPITAL GAIN AND CASH FLOW

KEY TERMS

- Depreciation allows owner of income property to deduct a portion of property's value from gross income each year over life of asset
- Basis is cost of a capital asset at a point in time
- Depreciable bases is undepreciated improvement portion of the property
- As property is depreciated, or new capital improvements are added, basis is adjusted accordingly and becomes a new adjusted basis
- If real estate sale proceeds exceed original cost, there is capital gain that is subject to tax
- If sale proceeds are less than original cost with adjustments, there is a capital loss
- An expense incurred by an income property that was paid to keep property operating and maintained is a tax deductible expense
- Taxable income from investment real estate is gross income received minus any expenses, deductions or exclusions that current tax law allows

CAPITAL GAIN ANALYSIS

- Capital gain on sale of property equal to amount from sale minus adjusted basis of home sold

Amount realized

- Net proceeds from sale
- Sale price - costs of sale = amount realized

Adjusted basis

- Beginning basis (amount invested in property) is increased or decreased by certain types of expenditures made while property is owned
- Beginning basis + capital improvements – depreciation = adjusted basis

Gain on sale

- Amount realized (net sales proceeds) – adjusted basis = gain on sale

INCOME PROPERTY CASH FLOW ANALYSIS

Steps in the cash flow analysis

- Identify pre-tax cash flow
- Identify tax liability
- Derive after-tax cash flow

Pre-tax cash flow   Cash flow before taxation

                                            potential rental income
-      vacancy and collection loss
=   effective rental income
+   other income
=   gross operating income

-      operating expenses
-      reserves
=   net operating income (NOI)
-      debt service
=   pre-tax cash flow

Tax liability
- Based on taxable income rather than cash flow
- Taxable income multiplied by owner's marginal tax bracket is tax liability

After-tax cash flow
- Amount of income from property that actually goes into owner's pocket after income tax is paid

Applying the analysis to investments
- Essential for investors to understand property's yield in relation to its value or price

==

Check Your Understanding Quiz:

Unit Twelve: Analysis of Capital Gain and Cash Flow

Carefully read each question then provide your best answer based on what you learned in this unit. Then check your answers against the Answer Key which immediately follows the quiz questions.

1. What is the name of an addition to a property that augments the property's value?

    a. Capital improvement
    b. Capital gain
    c. Appreciating basis
    d. Improvement basis

2. How do you calculate rate of return?

    a. Multiply the income by the price.
    b. Add the capital gains to the income.
    c. Divide the income by the price.
    d. Subtract the expenses from the net profit.

3. _____ is a measurement of how much is invested in the property for tax purposes.

    a. Growth
    b. Appreciation
    c. Gain
    d. Basis

4. What is the first step cash flow analysis?

    a. Identifying the tax liability
    b. Deriving the after-tax cash flow
    c. Identifying the potential and effective income
    d. Calculating the operating expenses

5. The net proceeds from a sale are also called the _____.

    a. amount realized.
    b. capital gains.
    c. gross profit.
    d. grown basis.

6. Which portion of real estate is depreciable?

    a. Land portion of real property
    b. Improvements on property
    c. Both the land and the improvements made on the property
    d. No portion of real estate is depreciable.

Answer Key:

Unit Twelve: Analysis of Capital Gain and Cash Flow

1. a. **Capital improvement**

2. **c. Divide the income by the price.**

3. **d. Basis**

4. **c. Identifying the potential and effective income**

5. **a. amount realized.**

6. **b. Improvements on property**

UNIT 13:

FLORIDA SALES CONTRACTS

Unit Thirteen Learning Objectives: When the student has completed this unit he or she will be able to:

- Explain how validity and enforceability of sales contracts are determined and what parties to the transaction are authorized to complete the sales contract.
- List and characterize the principal disclosures that must be made to the buyer and/or seller in completing the contracting process
- Summarize the general process and mechanics involved in finalizing an executed sales contract including offering, counteroffering, acceptance, contingencies and provisions for default
- Highlight essential provisions included in Florida sales contracts including deposits, possession, and default.

The Florida Real Estate Sales Contract is essential for all real estate agents to understand. Currently, two versions are used by real estate agents in the State of Florida: the Florida FAR/BAR As-Is contract and the CRSP-16 contract. The Florida Realtors and the Florida Bar Association have approved both versions. Agents must understand the various provisions of the contracts and the law behind them.

This unit will review these important terms and concepts. It will then review the provision and sections of the Florida Sales and Purchase contract, and the areas they should review with their customers. Finally, it will introduce some of the more commonly used sales contract addenda.

LEGAL CHARACTERISTICS

Validity and Enforceability

To be an enforceable contract in the State of Florida, a real estate contract must have five essential elements:

- Competent parties – parties must be of legal age and with sound mental capacity
- Offer and acceptance – there must be a clear meeting of the minds
- Legal purpose – the contract must represent an agreement to perform a legal act
- In writing – contracts must be in writing as required by the Statute of Frauds for all transfers of a real property interest
- Consideration – the contract must exchange something of value (good or valuable consideration) between both parties

Executory, Executed and Executing

There are three types of contracts in terms of their current or future performance: executory, executed and executing. A sales contract is **executory** when the signatories have yet to perform their respective obligations and promises. After closing, the contract becomes **executed** since all parties have done what they promised to do.

The real estate industry also uses the term **executing** a contract which is the process of the final signing of the contract by the principal parties.

To illustrate these phases, an agent shows a piece of property, and the buyers want to make an offer. The seller accepts the offer, and while the parties are signing the contract, they are executing the contract. During this process, the contract is only a verbal contract and can be canceled by either party. Critically, once both parties have signed the contract, it is an executory contract. The parties have yet to perform the duties and obligations they promised in the contract. After closing, it becomes an executed contract.

Completion by licensee

A broker may assist a buyer and seller in the completion of an offer to purchase. It is advisable and legally required in Florida for an agent to use the fill-in-the-blank contract promulgated by the Florida Realtors and approved by the Florida Bar or Florida Supreme Court. This relieves the broker of the dangers of creating new contract language, which can be seen as the practice of law.

Unauthorized Practice of Law

Real estate licensee drafting of contracts, riders, or addenda to contracts constitutes the unauthorized practice of law. Agents are prohibited from preparing any legal documents regarding the transaction, such as a deed, a title-related document, or mortgage documents. They are also barred from conducting real estate closings and providing legal advice.

Finally, agents are prohibited from having a principal party sign a contract with blanks to be completed later. Changes or deletions in a contract should only be made at the direction of the party signing the contract and must be initialed or signed, and dated. A licensee should advise a party who is unsure regarding any legal issue to contact an attorney.

CONTRACT-RELATED DISCLOSURES

There are certain disclosures that agents are required by law to give to their customers. Listed as follows are a few of the most important disclosures that must be made.

Commissions

An agent is required to disclose to all principal parties who is paying his or her commission and the commission amount. Agents are supposed to accept commissions or compensation from only one party of the transaction. Generally, the seller pays the broker's commission. It is important to put it in the notes section of the contract if there is a Buyer's Broker Agreement in place requiring a principal party to pay all or portions of the buyer agent's commission.

An agent is not allowed to pay any unlicensed person a commission. The only exception to this is if the agent is giving part of their commission to the buyer or the seller. If the agent plans to do this, it must be communicated to all parties before closing.

Property condition disclosure

Any known, material property defects must be disclosed to all parties. The Florida Supreme Court has ruled (in *Johnson versus Davis*) that the seller and the agents must disclose all known material defects that affect the property's value but are not readily observable.

For example, if there is a leak in the roof, this must be disclosed to the buyer even if the leak has done little or no damage to the property.

Homeowner's association disclosure

Any agent who sells a piece of property that falls under a mandatory Homeowner's Association (HOA), per Florida Statue 720, must give disclosure of the HOA to the buyer. Florida law requires specific disclosure that includes the HOA's existence, any fees required by the HOA, and rules that govern the HOA.

The contract or agreement must also include in prominent language a statement that the buyer should not execute the contract until the disclosure summary has been received and read. The contract must further state that the buyer may cancel the contract with a written notice within three days after receiving the summary and before closing. This right of rescission applies when the buyer's disclosure summary was not provided before contract execution. This right to cancel may not be waived.

Selling with an interest

Any agent who is selling their own property or property with which they have an interest in must disclose such a fact upon the "first meaningful contact." The Florida Real Estate Commission (FREC) has defined "first meaningful contact" to mean prior to entering into a listing contract or before showing the property. Failure to disclose an agent's interest may result in a complaint being filed with FREC.

The underlying issue is that an agent has an unfair advantage over the average buyer and seller, given his or her specialized real estate education, knowledge of the process and negotiation skills. This disclosure gives a buyer or seller an opportunity to get representation to theoretically "level the playing field."

Disclosure of stigmatized properties not required

Agents cannot be held legally responsible for failing to disclose stigmatized property. Stigmatized property is a property where someone has died, been murdered, or committed suicide. It also includes property that is presumed haunted.

Agents are not required to disclose the fact that anyone in a home has HIV or AIDs. Generally speaking, licensees should not disclose any medical information concerning the occupants of a home.

CONTRACTING MECHANICS AND PROCESS

Offer and acceptance

A contract of sale is created by the *full and unequivocal* acceptance of an offer. Offer and acceptance may come from either the buyer or the seller. The offeree must accept the offer without making any changes whatsoever. A change terminates the offer and creates a new offer or counteroffer. An offeror may revoke an offer for any reason before the communication of acceptance by the offeror.

Earnest money deposits

In Florida, earnest money is not a requirement to form a Sales and Purchase contract. The Florida Supreme Court has ruled that the offering and counteroffering process agents go through is enough consideration to create the contract. However, an agent does want to obtain an earnest money deposit because it provides potential compensation as liquidated damages for the seller if the buyer fails to perform. It also shows that the buyer is serious about buying the property if they are willing to commit to an earnest money deposit.

The sales contract provides the escrow instructions for handling and disbursing escrow funds. The earnest money is placed in the broker's trust account or a third-party's trust or escrow account, such as that of a title company or approved attorney. The deposit money is applied to the sales price at closing and lowers the amount of money the buyer must bring to the closing table.

Trust fund handling

Florida law prescribes how licensees must handle any escrow or earnest money deposits they receive. The broker or trust holder is required to place the funds in his or her trust account within the required time periods.

The Florida Sales and Purchase Contract requires inclusion of the name, address, and phone number of the company holding the escrow deposit. This inclusion must be very prominently placed on the first page of the contract.

Document distribution

Once all parties have signed the contract, copies should be distributed to the buyer and the seller. A copy also needs to go to the closing agent. This allows them to get started on the title search for the Opinion of Title or the Abstract of Title. Proper and timely document distribution is required by Florida law.

Contingencies

Most sales contracts contain one or more contingencies. A contingency is a condition that must be met within a time frame before the contract can be successfully fulfilled. The most common contingency concerns financing and inspections. A buyer makes an offer contingent on certain terms being met within a specific period of time. For example, a property inspection may need to be completed within ten days of the contract date. If it is completed and problems are found, the buyer can renegotiate the contract or cancel it without penalty. If the inspection is not performed within that time period, the buyer must accept the property as is or default on the contract.

Both buyers and sellers can abuse contingencies to leave themselves a convenient way to cancel without defaulting. To avoid problems, the statement of a contingency should

- be explicit and clear
- have an expiration date
- expressly require diligence in the effort to fulfill the requirements

A contingency that is too broad, vague, or excessive in duration may invalidate the entire contract on the grounds that there is an insufficiency of mutual agreement.

Default

A sale contract is bilateral since both parties promise to perform. As a result, either party may default by failing to perform. Note that a party's failure to meet a contingency does not constitute default but entitles the parties to cancel the contract.

Remedies for default by either party include:

- Liquidated damages to the seller – usually the buyer's earnest money deposit.
- Specific performance by either party – the parties must go through with the sale as agreed in the contract.
- Rescission of contract by either party – the parties are put back to their original positions, and the contract is canceled.
- Compensatory damages – any additional money that either principal has lost. For example, upgrades already completed on the property before the contract default.

KEY CONTRACT PROVISIONS

A typical residential sales and purchase contract contains the following primary provisions.

Parties, consideration, and property. One or more clauses will identify the parties, the property, and the consideration.

Parties. There must be at least two parties to the sales contract: the buyer and the seller. All parties must be identified, be of legal age, and have the capacity to contract. Also, if the parties are husband and wife, this is usually identified on the contract.

Property. A legal description sufficient for a competent surveyor to identify the property must be included in the contract. Generally, the postal address and the property appraisal parcel number are also included in the contract.

In addition to the real property location, any personal property that will be transferred with the property needs to be identified. The contract already states what fixtures will transfer with the property. The principal parties are free to add or delete what items are to be included in the sale. Whatever personal property items are staying or not staying with the property should be identified in the contract.

Consideration. Consideration in the contract is the purchase price. Also identified is the amount of earnest money being held. Also, expressly stated will be how the buyer intends to hold title – whether severally (individually), jointly, or as a tenant in common. In addition, the contract will detail what type of deed will be used to effect the transfer. The type of deed basically indicates what assurances the seller is giving as to the marketability of title and whether he or she will defend his or her ownership against any claims against the title being conveyed. Commonly, in Florida, unless otherwise stated in the contract, the buyer will get a General Warranty Deed.

Terms. The selling terms detail how the buyer is going to pay for the property purchase. It will indicate out the type of financing the buyer plans to get, the time frame given for securing the financing, the amount of funding the seller needs, and the interest rate they are willing to accept.

It is important for the agent to include all the acceptable terms in the contract. Failure to put in a maximum interest rate or the exact amount of financing needed could put the buyers in a situation where they must accept bank financing at a higher interest rate than intended.

Loan approval. A financing contingency clause states under what conditions the buyer can cancel the contract without default and receive a refund of the earnest money. If the buyer cannot secure the stated financing by the deadline, the parties may agree to extend the contingency by renegotiating and initializing new deadline dates entered into the contract. However, in the absence of timely renegotiation, not meeting the contract's deadlines makes the contract voidable where the seller can cancel the contract.

Escrow. The escrow clause provides for the custody and disbursement of the earnest money deposit. It also releases the escrow agent from certain liabilities in the performance of legitimate escrow duties.

An earnest money-related clause specifies how the buyer will pay the earnest money and when the deposits will be given to the escrow holder. Occasionally, additional deposits may be due. For example, a buyer who wants to buy a house can make an initial deposit of $200, to be followed in twenty-four hours with an additional $2,000.

Closing and possession dates. The contract states when the title will transfer and when the buyer will take physical possession. Customarily, possession occurs on the date when the deed is signed unless the buyer has agreed to other arrangements. The closing clause generally describes what must take place at closing to avoid default. The seller must provide clear and marketable title. The buyer must produce acceptably liquid purchase funds such as a cashier's check. Failure to complete any pre-closing requirements stated in the sale contract constitutes default and grounds for the aggrieved party to seek recourse.

Conveyed interest and type of deed. One or more provisions will state what kind of deed the seller will use to convey the property and what conditions the deed will be subject to. Among common "subject to" conditions are easements, association memberships, encumbrances, mortgages, liens, and special assessments. Typically, the seller conveys a fee simple interest utilizing a general warranty deed.

Title evidence. The seller agrees to produce the best possible proof of property ownership. This is most commonly in the form of title insurance in Florida. If the seller is not going to pay for the title insurance, this needs to be written in the contract notes section.

It is important to remember that anything written or added to the contract *supersedes* anything typed or part of the standard contract.

Closing costs. The contract identifies which closing costs each party will pay. Customarily, the seller pays title-related transfer costs, commissions, and property-related costs. The buyer typically pays financing-related costs. Annual property costs and revenue items such as taxes and rent are prorated between the parties. Note that who pays any closing cost is an item for negotiation.

Damage and destruction. This clause stipulates the obligations of the parties in case the property is damaged or destroyed prior to closing. The parties may negotiate alternatives, including seller's obligations to repair, buyer's obligations to buy if repairs are made, and the option for either party to cancel.

Seller's representation. Here the seller warrants that there will be no liens on the property that cannot be settled and extinguished at closing. Also, the seller warrants that all representations are accurate, and if found otherwise, the buyer may cancel the contract and reclaim the deposit.

SECONDARY CONTRACT PROVISIONS

A sales contract may contain numerous additional clauses, depending on the complexity of the transaction. The following summarizes the most important of these provisions.

Inspections. The parties agree to inspections and remedial action based on findings.

Owner's Association disclosure. This is the seller's disclosure of the existence of an association and the obligations it imposes.

Survey. This provides for a survey to satisfy financing requirements.

Compliance with laws. Here the seller warrants that there are no undisclosed building code or zoning violations.

Due-on-sale clause. This is an attest by the principals that any loans that survive the closing may be called due by the lender. Both parties agree to hold the other party harmless for the consequences of an acceleration of any underlying loan that survived closing.

Seller financing disclosure. Here the parties agree to comply with applicable state and local disclosure laws concerning seller financing.

Rental property and tenants' rights. In this provision, the buyer acknowledges the rights of tenants following closing.

FHA or VA financing condition. This is a contingency that allows the buyer to cancel the contract if the price exceeds FHA or VA estimates of the property's value.

Flood plain and insurance. Here the seller discloses that the property is in a flood plain and must carry flood insurance if the buyer uses certain lenders for financing.

Condominium assessments. The seller discloses assessments the owner must pay.

Foreign seller withholding. In this clause, the seller acknowledges that the buyer must withhold 15% of the purchase price at closing if the seller is a foreign person or entity. (FIRPTA) Further, the buyer will forward the withheld amount to the Internal Revenue Service. Certain limitations and exemptions apply.

Merger of agreements. Here the buyer and seller state that there are no other agreements between the parties that are not expressed in the contract.

Time is of the essence. The parties agree that they can amend dates and deadlines only if they both give written approval.

Survival. The parties continue to be liable for the truthfulness of representations and warranties after the closing.

Dispute resolution. The parties agree to resolve disputes through mediation and/or arbitration as opposed to court proceedings.

SNAPSHOT REVIEW: UNIT THIRTEEN

FLORIDA SALES CONTRACTS

LEGAL CHARACTERISTICS

Validity and enforceability
- to be enforceable, contract must meet validity criteria and be in writing
- validity = mutual consent; consideration; legal purpose; competent parties; voluntary act
- must identify principals, property with legal description, the price, must be signed.

Written vs. oral
- all sale contracts must be in writing per Florida Statutes of Fraud

Completion by a licensee
- licensee may complete a pre-approved fill-in-the-blank contract approved by Florida Realtors and Florida Bar Association.

CONTRACT-RELATED DISCLOSURES

Commission
- agents should disclose who is paying, how much they are getting paid
- should also disclose if sharing commission with buyer or seller.

Property condition
- all parties must disclose any known material property defects affecting the value.

HOA disclosure and fees
- agents must disclose in writing if there is a Homeowner's Association, fees

Selling with interest
- agent must disclose whether he or she has an interest in the property to all parties

Stigmatized properties
- need not disclose murders or suicides or a person's health status including AIDS or HIV

CONTRACTING MECHANICS AND PROCESS

Offer and Acceptance
- necessary to create a binding agreement
- it cannot make any changes to offer in order to create acceptance
- if changed, offer becomes a counteroffer.

Earnest money deposits
- not required in Florida
- deposits show buyer is serious; give protection to the seller in case of a default
- amount of escrow deposit varies
- title company or an attorney may also hold escrow funds

Trust fund handling
- broker must keep trust funds in a trust account until closing unless otherwise authorized by all parties

Document distribution
- copies of all documents must be distributed to all parties once signed

Contingencies
- contingencies must be satisfied before closing
- should be specific with duration deadline noted since they can trigger cancellation by either party.

Default
- seller retains the deposit as liquidated damages if buyer defaults
- seller can opt for other remedies if stated in agreement.
- broker may receive portions of the liquidated damages; seller may also sue for damages or specific performance.

KEY CONTRACT PROVISIONS

Parties, consideration, and property
- consideration is the property in exchange for the price
- must be at least two parties of legal age and mental capacity to contract
- property provision includes fixtures and personal property to be included.

Price and Terms
- the price and terms clause covers how the property will be paid for
- includes down payment and all specifics of the loan
- loan approval provision details any financing contingency and what happens if buyer is not approved.

Closing, possession, and deed
- contract stipulates the date of closing, move-in date, deed the seller will use
- seller must deliver clear, marketable title at closing with no unwanted or undisclosed encumbrances
- in Florida, seller must deliver a General Warranty Deed unless otherwise stated.

SECONDARY CONTRACT PROVISIONS

Clause descriptions
- inspections, homeowner's association disclosures, survey, environmental hazard disclosures, building code compliance, due-on-sale clause, seller financing disclosures, flood plain disclosure requiring flood insurance, condo assessment disclosure, foreign seller withholding requirements

===

Check Your Understanding Quiz:

Unit Thirteen: Florida Sales Contracts

Carefully read each question, then provide your best answer based on what you learned in this unit. Then check your answers against the Answer Key, which immediately follows the quiz questions.

1. A legal description must be sufficient for a competent _____ to identify the property.

    a. surveyor
    b. title agent
    c. escrow agent
    d. lender

2. A sales contract is _____ if the signatories have yet to perform their respective obligations and promises.

    a. fully performed
    b. a non-binding agreement
    c. completed
    d. executory

3. What happens if a buyer fails to perform his or her duties in a contract?

    a. Since a sale contract is unilateral it only requires that the seller perform.
    b. The contract may go into default.
    c. The seller cannot seek legal recourse for damages.
    d. The seller cannot sue for specific performance.

4. Which costs are typically covered by the buyer?

    a. The buyer's financing-related costs
    b. Title-related costs
    c. Property-related costs
    d. The total annual property tax amount

5. If the seller is a foreign person, the buyer must withhold _____ of the purchase price at closing and forward the withheld amount to the IRS.

    a. 10%
    b. 15%
    c. 20%
    d. 25%

6. Which of the following is the most common type of contingency?

    a. Code compliance contingency
    b. Appraisal contingency
    c. Financing contingency
    d. Sales of buyer's property contingency

==

Answer Key:

Unit Thirteen: Florida Sales Contracts

1. a. surveyor

2. d. executory

3. b. The contract may go into default.

4. a. The buyer's financing-related cost

5. b. 15%

6. c.   Financing contingency

Interactive Exercises

Unit 13: Florida Sales Contract

"AS IS" Residential Contract For Sale And Purchase
THIS FORM HAS BEEN APPROVED BY THE FLORIDA REALTORS AND THE FLORIDA BAR

FloridaRealtors®

1* PARTIES: _____ ("Seller"),
2* and _____ ("Buyer"),
3   agree that Seller shall sell and Buyer shall buy the following described Real Property and Personal Property
4   (collectively "Property") pursuant to the terms and conditions of this AS IS Residential Contract For Sale And Purchase
5   and any riders and addenda ("Contract"):
6   1. **PROPERTY DESCRIPTION:**
7*   (a) Street address, city, zip: _____
8*   (b) Located in: _____ County, Florida. Property Tax ID #: _____
9*   (c) Real Property: The legal description is _____
10   _____
11   _____
12   together with all existing improvements and fixtures, including built-in appliances, built-in furnishings and
13   attached wall-to-wall carpeting and flooring ("Real Property") unless specifically excluded in Paragraph 1(e) or
14   by other terms of this Contract.
15   (d) Personal Property: Unless excluded in Paragraph 1(e) or by other terms of this Contract, the following items
16   which are owned by Seller and existing on the Property as of the date of the initial offer are included in the
17   purchase: range(s)/oven(s), refrigerator(s), dishwasher(s), disposal, ceiling fan(s), intercom, light fixture(s),
18   drapery rods and draperies, blinds, window treatments, smoke detector(s), garage door opener(s), security gate
19   and other access devices, and storm shutters/panels ("Personal Property").
20*   Other Personal Property items included in this purchase are: _____
21   _____
22   Personal Property is included in the Purchase Price, has no contributory value, and shall be left for the Buyer.
23*   (e) The following items are excluded from the purchase: _____
24   _____

25   PURCHASE PRICE AND CLOSING

26* 2. **PURCHASE PRICE** (U.S. currency):... $_____
27*   (a) Initial deposit to be held in escrow in the amount of **(checks subject to COLLECTION)** .... $_____
28   The initial deposit made payable and delivered to "Escrow Agent" named below
29*   **(CHECK ONE):** (i) ☐ accompanies offer or (ii) ☐ is to be made within _____ (if left
30   blank, then 3) days after Effective Date. IF NEITHER BOX IS CHECKED, THEN
31   OPTION (ii) SHALL BE DEEMED SELECTED.
32*   Escrow Agent Information: Name: _____
33*   Address: _____
34*   Phone: _____ E-mail: _____ Fax: _____
35*   (b) Additional deposit to be delivered to Escrow Agent within _____ (if left blank, then 10)
36*   days after Effective Date .... $_____
37   (All deposits paid or agreed to be paid, are collectively referred to as the "Deposit")
38*   (c) Financing: Express as a dollar amount or percentage ("Loan Amount") see Paragraph 8 .... _____
39*   (d) Other: _____ .... $_____
40   (e) Balance to close (not including Buyer's closing costs, prepaids and prorations) by wire
41*   transfer or other **COLLECTED** funds .... $_____
42   **NOTE: For the definition of "COLLECTION" or "COLLECTED" see STANDARD S.**
43   3. **TIME FOR ACCEPTANCE OF OFFER AND COUNTER-OFFERS; EFFECTIVE DATE:**
44   (a) If not signed by Buyer and Seller, and an executed copy delivered to all parties on or before
45*   _____, this offer shall be deemed withdrawn and the Deposit, if any, shall be returned to
46   Buyer. Unless otherwise stated, time for acceptance of any counter-offers shall be within 2 days after the day
47   the counter-offer is delivered.
48   (b) The effective date of this Contract shall be the date when the last one of the Buyer and Seller has signed or
49   initialed and delivered this offer or final counter-offer ("Effective Date").
50   4. **CLOSING DATE:** Unless modified by other provisions of this Contract, the closing of this transaction shall occur
51   and the closing documents required to be furnished by each party pursuant to this Contract shall be delivered
52*   ("Closing") on _____ ("Closing Date"), at the time established by the Closing Agent.

"AS IS" Residential Contract For Sale And Purchase
THIS FORM HAS BEEN APPROVED BY THE FLORIDA REALTORS AND THE FLORIDA BAR

1* **PARTIES:** _____ John and Jane Doe (H/W) _____ ("Seller"),
2* and _____ Sally Smith _____ ("Buyer"),
3 agree that Seller shall sell and Buyer shall buy the following described Real Property and Personal Property
4 (collectively "Property") pursuant to the terms and conditions of this AS IS Residential Contract For Sale And Purchase
5 and any riders and addenda ("Contract"):
6 **1. PROPERTY DESCRIPTION:**
7*   (a) Street address, city, zip: _____ 321 Main Street, Anytown, FL 32001 _____
8*   (b) Located in: _____Brevard_____ County, Florida. Property Tax ID #: _____987652_____
9*   (c) Real Property: The legal description is Lot 5, Block 2 of the Anytown Subdivision as recorded in Book 10,
10   Page 325 in the Brevard County Records
11
12   together with all existing improvements and fixtures, including built-in appliances, built-in furnishings and
13   attached wall-to-wall carpeting and flooring ("Real Property") unless specifically excluded in Paragraph 1(e) or
14   by other terms of this Contract.
15   (d) Personal Property: Unless excluded in Paragraph 1(e) or by other terms of this Contract, the following items
16   which are owned by Seller and existing on the Property as of the date of the initial offer are included in the
17   purchase: range(s)/oven(s), refrigerator(s), dishwasher(s), disposal, ceiling fan(s), intercom, light fixture(s),
18   drapery rods and draperies, blinds, window treatments, smoke detector(s), garage door opener(s), security gate
19   and other access devices, and storm shutters/panels ("Personal Property").
20*   Other Personal Property items included in this purchase are: _Fans, hot tub, washer, and dryer_
21
22   Personal Property is included in the Purchase Price, has no contributory value, and shall be left for the Buyer.
23*   (e) The following items are excluded from the purchase: _refrigerator_
24

25   **PURCHASE PRICE AND CLOSING**

26* **2. PURCHASE PRICE** (U.S. currency):... $ 120,000.00

27*   (a) Initial deposit to be held in escrow in the amount of **(checks subject to COLLECTION)** .... $ 5,000.00
28   The initial deposit made payable and delivered to "Escrow Agent" named below
29*   **(CHECK ONE):** (i) [x] accompanies offer or (ii) [ ] is to be made within _____ (if left
30   blank, then 3) days after Effective Date. IF NEITHER BOX IS CHECKED, THEN
31   OPTION (ii) SHALL BE DEEMED SELECTED.
32*   Escrow Agent Information: Name: _____ Anytown Title Company _____
33*   Address: _____ 890 Main Street, Anytown, FL 32001 _____
34*   Phone: _555-888-1212_ E-mail: _Anytowntitle@gmail.com_ Fax: _555-888-1213_
35*   (b) Additional deposit to be delivered to Escrow Agent within ____10____ (if left blank, then 10)
36*   days after Effective Date ....$ 5,000.00
37   (All deposits paid or agreed to be paid, are collectively referred to as the "Deposit")
38*   (c) Financing: Express as a dollar amount or percentage ("Loan Amount") see Paragraph 8 .... _$80,000.00_
39*   (d) Other: _____ Seller Financing _____ $ 20,000.00
40   (e) Balance to close (not including Buyer's closing costs, prepaids and prorations) by wire
41*   transfer or other **COLLECTED** funds ....$ 10,000.00
42   **NOTE:** For the definition of "COLLECTION" or "COLLECTED" see STANDARD S.
43 **3. TIME FOR ACCEPTANCE OF OFFER AND COUNTER-OFFERS; EFFECTIVE DATE:**
44   (a) If not signed by Buyer and Seller, and an executed copy delivered to all parties on or before
45*   _____March 8, 2021_____, this offer shall be deemed withdrawn and the Deposit, if any, shall be returned to
46   Buyer. Unless otherwise stated, time for acceptance of any counter-offers shall be within 2 days after the day
47   the counter-offer is delivered.
48   (b) The effective date of this Contract shall be the date when the last one of the Buyer and Seller has signed or
49   initialed and delivered this offer or final counter-offer ("Effective Date").
50 **4. CLOSING DATE:** Unless modified by other provisions of this Contract, the closing of this transaction shall occur
51   and the closing documents required to be furnished by each party pursuant to this Contract shall be delivered
52*   ("Closing") on _____April 30, 2021_____ ("Closing Date"), at the time established by the Closing Agent.

FloridaRealtors/FloridaBar-ASIS-5x   Rev 6/19 © 2017 Florida Realtors® and The Florida Bar. All rights reserved.

Serial# 030096-800161-5909115

Form
Simplicity

UNIT 14:

PRE-CLOSING AND CLOSING

Unit Fourteen Learning Objectives: When the student has completed this unit he or she will be able to:

- Describe the essential tasks and diligence that must be performed following contracting and preceding closing, including financing, inspections, and repairs.
- Describe the key events that must transpire at closing and what roles the broker, lender and principals play in completing the closing process
- Summarize the key provisions of RESPA / TRID in closing residential transactions.
- Describe and quantify real estate taxes charged at closing including the prorated ad valorem tax, stamp tax, doc stamp tax and intangible tax

PRE-CLOSING LOGISTICS AND TASKS

The Sales and Purchase Contract of a given transaction sets forth the duties, schedules, and responsibilities of each contracting party. The contract assumes that both parties are satisfied with the binding terms of the contract. The contract is legally enforceable only when all validity criteria of the contract have been satisfied, and the buyer and seller have signed the contract.

Sales Associate responsibilities

The sales associate is responsible for assisting in negotiating the contract and ensuring that the contract is completed properly. The sales associate should also go over all the required disclosures and ensure each party understands what they must pay. Each party should estimate how much money they will need to bring to closing or how much they will receive from the closing.

If the sales associate receives an escrow deposit, it needs to be delivered to the broker by the end of the next business day if the broker is to hold the deposit. If a closing agent is involved, the deposit and a copy of the contract should be delivered to such closing agent as soon as possible.

The sales associate's responsibility is to ensure all contingencies in the contract are met and completed in the timeframe laid out in the contract. If a contingency is not completed on time, the contract becomes voidable by the other party unless both parties sign an extension, and a new completion date is established.

Broker responsibilities

The broker is required to ensure the sales associate has properly completed the sales contract. If the broker holds the escrow deposit, he or she should ensure it is deposited in a trust account within three days of receiving it from the sales associate. Typically, a broker will only become involved in the negotiation or execution of a contract if the sales associate runs into problems.

In Florida, most closings are completed at a title company or by a Florida real estate attorney. Thus, once the broker has reviewed the contract, he or she will leave the rest of the details for the title company and the sales associate to complete. The only other duty the broker would be required to perform is to transfer any escrow deposits to the closing agent before closing. This falls under the broker's duty to account for all funds.

Inspections

Most closings are contingent on the property meeting certain condition criteria. Meeting property condition requirements is one of the most important steps in the closing process. This is the only way the buyer can ensure that there are no major problems with the property. If something major is found, the contract may need to be renegotiated, or depending on how the contract is written, the buyers may be able to void the contract and get their escrow deposit back. It is important that, even with an "As-Is" contract, timely property inspections are completed in order to determine what issues exist and what the costs are to complete any repairs.

In Florida, a licensed home inspector is hired to do the inspection. The home inspector will check the home's structure and all systems on the property, such as plumbing, electric, HVAC, etc. Most inspectors give the buyers and their agent a detailed and photo-supported explanation of what they found in the home inspection.

Loan approval

A buyer who plans to finance the home purchase must obtain a mortgage loan before completing the purchase transaction. The contract usually sets out the buyer's timeframe for their loan and how long they have to get loan approval.

Most transactions allow for the contract to be contingent on the buyer's obtaining conventional or FHA financing for the purchase. Since loan approval is typically a contingency within the purchase contract, the seller should be notified when the approval is obtained or denied.

Problems with getting financing through the bank's underwriters are the number one reason why delays in closing may occur. The sales associate should ensure that the parties have allowed enough time to get the loan approved when setting the closing date. If they cannot meet the documented closing date because the financing has not been approved, the contract must be extended or terminated by the seller.

The sales associate should use care when completing the contract's financing section and include the exact amount of money the buyer needs to close the deal and the maximum amount of interest the buyer is willing to pay. If the financing section is completed properly, the buyer can get out of the contract and get their escrow deposit back if the contract terms cannot be met.

Other contingencies

The purchase contract usually contains several different contingencies to the purchase. The most typical contingencies include the following

- the buyer obtaining financing
- the buyer performing a home inspection and, if needed, a "wood-destroying organism" inspection
- the seller's disclosure of all known material facts that can affect the home's value
- the seller's completing any agreed-upon repairs
- the buyer's right to cancel the contract based on the results of the inspection
- the home appraising for the sales price or higher
- the title search being completed with the result being unclouded, marketable title
- a survey that clears any encumbrances not already identified

Final preparations to closing

All buyers should complete a final walk-through inspection on the day of closing. This ensures all fixtures and personal property listed on the contract remain with the property and that no damage was done to the property when the seller moved out.

For example, during a condominium's final walk-through, the buyer discovered that the seller had stripped the unit of numerous fixtures that normally run with the property. All interior doors, window dressings, lights, electrical switches, and even the toilet paper holders were gone. According to the contract, all these items were to convey with the property. The buyer's agent notified the seller's agent and gave the seller until 4:00 p.m. that day to replace all the items with no damage to the property, or the contract would be voided.

The buyer should also review the Closing Disclosure Statement (CD) with their sales associate to ensure all CD charges are in accord with charges indicated in the Sales Contract. The buyer should then wire-transfer the final amount due to the closing agent.

Care should be taken when wiring the purchase funds, as mortgage fraud has become an increasingly prevalent occurrence in Florida. For example, one common fraud tactic is to send the buyer a phony email from what appears to be the title company. The email states that the routing number and account number on the first email has changed due to banking errors. It then gives new routing numbers and account numbers to wire the money to. Often, the new numbers will be to a country where the money cannot be traced or recovered.

If the broker is holding any escrow money, this should be transferred to the title company before closing. Most title companies will not distribute any funds until they have all money from the sale in their escrow account. Most title companies prefer that all money for the transaction come to them, and all expenses and proceeds get paid out by them.

CLOSING ESSENTIALS

The settlement process

The closing process consists of the buyer and the seller verifying that each has fulfilled the terms of the sale contract. If they have, then at closing, the mortgage loan, if any, is closed and those funds transferred to the title company. All expenses are apportioned and paid, the consideration is exchanged for the title, all final documents are signed, and arrangements are made to record the transaction according to local laws.

Title transfer and funds transfer

In order to close, the seller must produce evidence of marketable title, as evidenced by title insurance, and the opinion of title or an affidavit of title. A clean, marketable title generally is a title without liens or claims on title that must be settled.

The seller may also be asked to execute an affidavit of title stating that, since the date of the original title search, the seller has incurred no new liens, judgments, unpaid bills for repairs or improvements, no unrecorded deeds or contracts, no bankruptcies or divorces that would after the title, or any other defects the seller is aware of.

One important step at closing is the voluntarily delivery and acceptance of the deed. In the past, this was completed with both parties at the closing table. The seller would sign the deed and push it across the table to the buyer. The buyer would then accept the deed, and the property would have legally transferred ownership. Today, title companies and real estate agents prefer to do separate closings. Typically, the sellers will come in first and sign their paperwork, including the deed. Then, the buyers come in and complete their paperwork. The closing agent will then push the signed deed across the table to the buyer. Once the buyer accepts the deed, the property is transferred.

Florida has just started allowing virtual closings. So now, if a buyer, seller, or both are not in the area and cannot come to the closing agent's office, the closing agent can witness the buyer and/or seller signing the documents on the computer. This helps cut down on the cost of sending out all the closing documents and ensuring they are properly completed and notarized.

Lender's requirements at closing

Before approving the loan, the lender will qualify the loan applicant and the property held as collateral for the loan. The collateral must not be endangered by

- defects in the title
- by liens that would take priority over the principal mortgage lien, such as property taxes
- by physical damage to the property if not repaired

To safeguard the property collateral, the lender typically requires

- a survey
- a property inspection
- hazard insurance
- a title insurance policy

- a reserve account for hazard insurance and property taxes
- if applicable, private mortgage insurance where there is insufficient equity in the down payment.

In some cases, the lender may also require occupancy certificates to verify that any new construction performed complies with local building codes.

Broker's role

The broker or sales associate usually continues to provide pre-closing services between the signing of the sale contract and the closing. This includes making arrangements for pre-closing activities such as inspections, surveys, appraisals, and repairs and generally taking steps to ensure that the closing can proceed as scheduled.

In Florida, the closing proceedings are usually conducted by a title company. Still, the broker or associate is expected to explain and verify entries on the closing documents as well as attend the closing with the buyer or seller. The broker or associate is also responsible for delivering the escrow check to the closing agent.

RESPA / TRID SYNOPSIS

Effective October 3, 2015, a Truth-in-Lending Act/ Real Estate Settlement Procedures Act (TILA/RESPA) developed the Integrated Disclosure Rule (TRID). This rule integrated the disclosure requirements of RESPA and the Truth-In-Lending Act. It also replaced the Good Faith Estimate form and the HUD-1 Uniform Settlement Statement with the new Loan Estimate form and the Closing Disclosure form, respectively.

This act's main purpose was to make the loan processes and costs more transparent to the consumer. Both documents clearly outline all the charges and expenses of the buyer's loan and the total amount the buyer will pay the lender over the life of the loan.

Information booklet

A lender subject to RESPA must give loan applicants the Consumer Financial Protection Bureau (CFPB) booklet, "Your Home Loan Toolkit," within three days of receiving a loan application. This booklet describes loans, closing costs, and the Closing Disclosure form.

Lender disclosures

At the time of loan application or within three business days of application, a lender must give the applicant a Loan Estimate (H-24) of likely settlement costs. This estimate is usually based on comparable transactions completed in the area. The terms stated in the subsequent Closing Disclosure must agree with those of the Loan Estimate within pre-set limits.

Mortgage servicing

The lender must disclose to the buyer whether the lender intends to service the loan or convey it to another loan-service organization for servicing. This disclosure must also be accompanied by information as to how the buyer can resolve complaints.

H-25 disclosures of settlement costs

Under CFPB rules, a lender must use the Closing Disclosure (H-25) to disclose settlement costs to the buyer. This form covers all costs that the buyer will have to pay at closing, whether to the lender or other parties. Use of this form enforces RESPA's prohibition against a lender's requiring a buyer to deposit an excessive amount in the tax and insurance escrow account or to use a particular title company for title insurance. The consumer must receive the completed form not later than three business days before closing. The consumer also has the right to inspect a revised form one business day before closing. A description and example of this form are provided later in this section.

Escrow disclosures

Loan servicers must provide borrowers with an annual escrow statement that summarizes all inflow and outflows in the prior 12-month period. The statement must also disclose shortfalls or overages in the account and how the discrepancies will be resolved.

Section 10 of RESPA limits the amounts lenders can require borrowers to place in escrow to pay taxes, hazard insurance, and other property-related expenses. The limitation applies to the initial deposits and deposits made over the course of the loan's terms. If the amount being held in the account is $50 or more at the end of the year, then the money must be returned to the buyer.

Referrals and kickback disclosures

RESPA prohibits the payment of fees as part of a real estate settlement when no services are rendered. This includes kickbacks or referral fees from any party directly involved in the closing, including the title company, real estate agents, lender, surveyor, attorney, or the appraiser.

PRORATIONS

Real estate agents must understand how to explain the Closing Disclosure statement to their customers. One item that agents have trouble with is prorations.

A proration is an expense or an income item where the buyer and seller pay or receive their pro rata share based on how much of the benefit of the payment (tax) or income (rent) they respectively enjoy. Take taxes for example. If a seller and buyer close two-thirds of the way through the year, the seller must pay taxes for that 2/3 period where he owned the property, and the buyer must pay for one-third where she owned the property. Since the taxes are paid in arrears, the buyer will receive the entire bill. To avoid the problem, the tax expense is simply apportioned to the parties at closing – and, specifically, the seller gets a charge and the buyer gets a credit for two-thirds of the tax bill that the buyer will receive at the end of the year.

To calculate a proration properly, an agent must understand who owns the day of closing. Per the standard contract in Florida, the day of closing belongs to the buyer. This means the buyer pays all expenses of the day of closing and earns all income of the day of closing. If the seller owns the day of closing, this must be added to the contract in the notes section.

For example, An apartment rents for $900 per month. The owner decides to sell the unit. The day of closing is April 14th. What proration would occur on the Closing Disclosure Statement? Assume the day of closing belongs to the buyer.

      $900 ÷ 30 days in April = $30 rent earned per day
      $30 x 17 buyer days = $510
      Credit buyer $510, Debit seller $510

Since we know the day of closing, we use the 365-day method of proration. The seller collects the rent on the 1st of the month, so the seller owes the buyer the rent for the days the buyer owns the house. The day of closing belongs to the buyer, so we count that day in our numbers.

The other proration method is the 360-day method. This method assumes that every month has 30 days in it, including February. This method is used if the closing date is unknown or the agent estimates the closing cost for the buyer or seller.

It is important to understand how items are paid. Some items such as property taxes and utilities are paid in arrears. At the closing time, the seller has incurred the expense, but the expenses have not been billed or paid yet. The buyer will have to pay the bill sometime after closing.

If an item is paid in arrears, the proration will be a credit to the buyer and a debit to the seller. The seller must pay the buyer for the time they owned the house. Example 2 shows property taxes that are paid in arrears.

Some items such as rent which the seller has already received, or HOA fees that the seller has already paid are known as advance fees. So, the buyer reimburses the seller for the time the buyer owns the home.

If an item is paid in advance, the proration will be a credit to the seller and a debit to the buyer. The previous example shows rent that was paid in advance.

Example 2: The annual property taxes on a property piece are estimated to run $2,236 for the current year. The date of closing is May 16th, and the day of closing belonging to the buyer. What would be the proration on the Closing Disclosure for the property taxes?

          $2236 ÷ 365 = $6.13
          J31 + F28 + M31 + A30 +M15 = 135 seller days
          135 days x $6.13 per day = $827.55
          Credit buyer $827.55, Debit seller $827.55

If an agent does not understand prorations, they should meet with their broker or a closing agent and explain the concept so they can explain them to the buyer or seller.

TAXES AT CLOSING

Transfer tax, or documentary stamp tax as it is referred to in Florida, is a tax imposed by states, counties, and cities to transfer the title of property from one person or entity to another. The common practice is for the seller to pay the Documentary Stamps on the Deed and are generally paid at a rate of $.70 per $100. This is true all over Florida except in Miami-Dade County, where it is paid at a rate of $.60 per $100. This is paid on the selling price of the house.

Documentary stamp tax on the promissory note is paid on all new notes or assumed notes. This is paid to add names to a note. It is generally paid at a rate of $.35 per $100 of the promissory note's price. Generally, the documentary stamp on the note is paid for by the buyer.

Intangible tax is paid on all new mortgages to record them in public records. It is only paid on new mortgages and not on assumed mortgages. It is paid at a rate of 2 mils (.002) on the new mortgage cost and is generally paid by the buyer.

Example: Calculate all applicable State Doc Stamps and Intangible taxes dues for recording the new instruments for the below transaction.

Selling Price	$150,000
Cash Binder Deposit	$ 5,000
ASSUME Existing 1st Mtg	$ 75,000
NEW PMM 2nd Mtg	$ 45,000
Cash at Closing	$ 25,000

$150,000 \div 100 = 1500 \ x .70 = $1,050$ Doc Stamp on the Deed (1st Mtg.)
$75,000 \div 100 = 750 \ x \ $.35 = 262.50 Doc Stamp on the Deed (2nd Mtg.)
$45,000 \ x .002 = 90.00 Intangible Tax on New Mortgage
$45,000 \div 100 = 450 \ x .35 = 157.50 Doc Stamp on the Note

$1,050 + $262.50 + $90.00 + $157.50 = **$1,560.00 Total Transfer Taxes**
$1,050 paid by the seller and $510 paid by the buyer

FORM H-25 REVIEW

The H-25 is commonly called the Closing Disclosure Statement (CD). The CD is a 5-page document where pages 1, 4, and 5 will change depending on the type of loan the buyer is getting. Real estate agents are generally concerned with pages 2 and 3. The following information is based on a 30-year fixed rate amortized mortgage:

Page 1 has four sections: general information about the lender and borrower, the property, and the type of loan, it states the projected payments and what is included in those payments, and the Costs at Closing.

Page 2 has four columns. It shows the expenses incurred by the buyer and seller. It also differentiates the expenses being paid during the closing process and those paid before closing.

Page 3 has two sections, one for calculating cash to close, the other to summarize the buyer and seller's transaction. It also compares the loan estimate costs to the actual costs. It also gives the final number for the closing, the amount of money the buyer must transfer to close, and how much the seller will get at closing.

Page 4 provides additional loan information such as escrow accounts, late payments, etc.

Page 5 provides additional calculations, disclosures, and contact information for the individual involved in the closing.

Agents are encouraged to familiarize themselves with the closing disclosures. They need to be able to explain the different parts of the CD to their buyer and seller. If they are uncomfortable explaining the CD, they should get a peer, their broker, or someone with a title company or lender to explain the CD to them.

==

SNAPSHOT REVIEW: UNIT FOURTEEN

UNIT 14: PRE-CLOSING AND CLOSING

PRE-CLOSING LOGISTICS AND TASKS

Sales Associate responsibilities
- sales associate responsible for ensuring contingencies are cleared in a timely manner.
- also typically schedule the inspection and survey.

Broker responsibilities
- broker responsible for ensuring the escrow deposit is handled legally.

Inspections
- home inspector should be hired to inspect property; usually one of the major contingencies to be fulfilled.
- Sales associate must make sure all repairs are completed before closing

Loan approval
- contract states when buyer must submit the loan application and deadline for getting loan approval - agent's responsibility to ensure these dates are met. If not met, the contract becomes voidable by seller.

Other contingencies
- survey, appraisal, financing terms.

CLOSING ESSENTIALS

The settlement process
- agents confirm all parties have fulfilled the terms of the contract
- principals exchange the consideration stated in the contract, sign all the required documentation.

Title transfer and funds transfer
- seller required to give a marketable title at closing; remove all liens or encumbrances necessary to deliver marketable title.

Lender's requirements at closing
- lender must provide all the documentation to close the loan.
- lender also ensures funds are released upon signing, verifying paperwork

Broker's role
- The broker's role in closing can vary; must at least make sure escrow deposit is delivered to the closing company before closing.

RESPA / TRID SYNOPSIS

Information booklet
- lender must provide borrower with the Consumer Financial Protection Bureau booklet, "Your Home Loan Toolkit."

Lender disclosures
- lender must provide the H-24 Loan Estimate within three days of the loan application being completed.

Mortgage servicing
- lender must let the borrower know who will be servicing the loan.

H-25 disclosures of settlement costs
- lender must use the CFPB's H-25 Closing Disclosure Statement to list all information about the loan and the settlement charges each party is paying.

Escrow disclosures
- Loan servicers must provide annual escrow statements to the borrowers.

Referrals and kickback disclosures
- RESPA prohibits payment of referral fees and kickbacks to anyone directly involved in the closure.
- also requires disclosure of business relations between firms involved in the transaction.

PRORATIONS

- Prorated items are income or expenses incurred by the buyer or the seller in advance or arrears.
- buyer and seller split the cost or income of a prorated item.
- Common prorations: property taxes, rent, mortgage interest, insurance premiums.

TAXES AT CLOSING

- The State requires Document Stamp Taxes on the Deed be paid by the seller at closing.
- rate is $.70 per $100 of the sales price.
- buyer pays document Stamp Taxes on the Note at closing at a rate of $.35 per $100. The buyer pays intangible Tax on the new mortgage at a rate of 2 mils of the mortgage value.

FORM H-25 REVIEW -- also known as the Closing Disclosure Statement.

===

Check Your Understanding Quiz:

Unit Fourteen: Pre-closing and Closing

Carefully read each question then provide your best answer based on what you learned in this unit. Then check your answers against the Answer Key which immediately follows the quiz questions.

1. Which of the following items are paid in arrears?

    a. Taxes and insurance
    b. Rent and interest
    c. Taxes and interest
    d. Rents and insurance

2. A prorated expense on the settlement statement is

    a. a debit to the buyer or seller
    b. a credit to the buyer or seller
    c. a debit and credit to the buyer and seller
    d. a debit to one party and a credit to the other

3. The Loan Estimate must be sent to the borrower within how many days of completing the loan application

    a. 3 days
    b. 10 days
    c. 15 days
    d. 30 days

4. The purpose of the closing event is to

    a. confirm that the buyer has fulfilled all contract requirements before title transfer immediately after closing
    b. ensure that the seller has a marketable title before the monies are transferred
    c. conclude the process for loan approval
    d. exchange legal title for the sale price

5. What is the intangible tax on a mortgage of $150,000 if the rate is 2 mils (.002)?

    a. $300.00
    b. $3,000.00
    c. $750.00
    d. $30.00

6. Which of the following are common contract contingencies?

    a. the closing date
    b. the date the escrow deposit is due
    c. the inspection
    d. who the closing agent will be

===

Answer Key:

Unit Fourteen: Pre-closing and Closing

1. **c. Taxes and interest**

2. **d. a debit to one party and a credit to the other**

3. **a. 3 days**

4. **d. exchange legal title for the sale price**

5. **a. $300**

6. **c. the inspection**

Interactive Exercises

Unit 14: Pre-closing and Closing

Case Problems: Prorations

Jeff and Michelle are buying a piece of investment property. The current tenant is paying $1,500 per month, and the current month's rent was paid on the 1st of the month. It is estimated that the property taxes on the property will run $2,750 this year. The day of closing is April 10th. According to the contract, the day of closing belongs to the buyer. Assume 30 days in April and a 365-day year.

Case study scenario question

1. What is the proration for this month's rent?
2. What is the proration for the property taxes?
3. Practice explaining the prorations to your buyer.

Case Debrief:

1. Rent Proration (Paid in Advance)

   $1,500 ÷ 30 days = $50 per day
   21 buyer days (rent counts the days the buyer owns the property)
   21 days x $50 rent per day = $1,050
   Debit Seller $1,050, Credit Buyer $1,050

   It is a debit to the seller because the seller has already received the rent and must pay (credit) the buyer for the days they own the apartment.

2. Property Tax (Paid in Arrears)

   $2,750 per year ÷ 365 days in a year = $7.53 per day
   J31 + F28 + M31 + A9 = 99 seller days
   99 seller days x $7.53 property taxes paid per day = $745.47
   Debit seller $745.47, Credit Buyer $745.47

   This is a debit to the seller because the buyer will pay the property tax bill at the end of the year. The seller must pay (debit) the buyer for the days the seller lives in the home. This way, the buyer has the money to pay the property taxes at the end of next year.

If you liked Florida Real Estate Continuing Education (FLA.CE), check out the other Florida titles of Performance Programs Company!

Needing to complete your 14 hours of CE? Performance Programs Company has you covered!

Where can you buy Performance Programs Company's 14-Hour Florida Real Estate Continuing Education (FLA.CE) program?
Our FLA.CE Program is available through licensed real estate schools

Looking to complete your Florida 45 sales postlicensing requirement? Go with Performance Programs Company's Florida Real Estate Postlicensing for Sales Associates!

Florida Real Estate Postlicensing for Sales Associates is a 45-hour review and applied principles course for newly-licensed sales associates beginning their real estate careers in Florida. Successful completion of this course will satisfy your one-time postlicense requirement as a sales associate actively practicing real estate in Florida.

Where can you buy Florida Real Estate Postlicensing for Sales Associates?
Florida Real Estate Postlicensing for Sales Associates is available as a printed book or e-book through nearly all online retailers.

Looking for a Florida-specific real estate principles textbook? Get what all the students love -- Principles of Real Estate Practice in Florida!

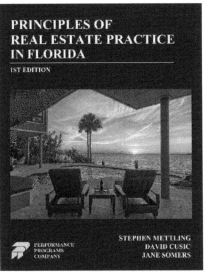

Principles of Real Estate Practice in Florida is invaluable reference material for real estate professionals. Its 525-pages contain the essentials of real estate law, principles, and practices taught in real estate schools and colleges across Florida.

Where can you buy Principles of Real Estate Practice in Florida?
Principles Real Estate Practice in Florida is available as a printed book or e-book through nearly all online retailers.

Cramming for the Florida real estate sales associate exam? You need Florida Real Estate License Exam Prep!

Where can you buy Florida Real Estate License Exam Prep?
Florida Real Estate License Exam Prep is available as a printed book or e-book through nearly all online retailers.

Publisher Contact
Ryan Mettling
Performance Programs Company
502 S. Fremont Ave., Ste. 724, Tampa, FL 33606
813-512-6269
ryan@performanceprogramscompany.com
www.performanceprogramscompany.com

Made in the USA
Columbia, SC
14 March 2022

57486825R00102